AWAKENING TO NATURE

A Practical and Meditative Journey through the Gardening Year

MICHAEL FULLER

GREEN MAGIC

Awakening to Nature © 2025 by Michael Fuller. All rights reserved. No part of this book may be used or reproduced in any form without written permission of the Author, except in the case of quotations in articles and reviews.

Green Magic
Seed Factory
Aller
Langport
Somerset
TA10 0QN
England
www.greenmagicpublishing.com

Designed and typeset by Carrigboy, Wells, UK
www.carrigboy.co.uk

Cover picture: *'Dandelion'* – Lil Tudor-Craig (*www.tudor-craig.co.uk*)
Cover design: Wolfie Wright

ISBN 978 1 915580 24 5

GREEN MAGIC

'… the Earth does not belong to man, man belongs to the Earth. This we know. All things are connected like the blood which unites one family. All things are connected. Whatever befalls the sons of Earth. Man did not weave the web of life; he is merely a strand in it. Whatever he does to the web he does to himself.'

From Chief Seattle's Testimony, 1850

CONTENTS

Introduction 9
A gardening wheel of the Year. 15

January: Beginnings
Witch Hazel – January's Winter bloom 19
The garden in January. 21
Winter pruning of apple and pear trees 23

February: The Light Returns
The garden in February 28
Our native daffodil – the Lent Lily 32
Rain in the garden 35
The union of intuition with intellect 39

March: The Time of Balance and Awakening
The Spring Equinox. 42
The art of 'incorrect' gardening 46
Rose pruning – 'no pain, no gain' 48
Eco-heaps revisited 53

April: Into Action
The compost heap – the 'heart chakra' of the
    garden 56
How green is your grass? – lawn mowing and
    climate change. 59
Weeding reconsidered 62
A simple vegetable plot 65
The hazel – beautiful, generous and useful 67

CONTENTS

May: Widening into Worldwide Life
The garden in May 70
Celandine – my favourite 'weed'. 72
Why we need to recognise plants as sovereign beings
    (Plant health part 1) 74

June: The Sun's High Hour
The garden in June 78
June – the month of the rose. 81
How can we help plants heal themselves?
    (Plant health part 2) 83

July: The Dance Changes
Efficient, ethical and cost effective – 10 garden tips
    for July 89
'What shall we do with all this rubbish?' – how to
    end the 'war on weeds' 94
No-mow May (… and June, July?). 97
Trees in the garden 99

August: Harvest
Lammas – the festival of first fruits 103
Movement is life – the garden in August 106
Compost – the heart of the garden. 110
Finding balance in the garden 114

September: Pausing at the Equinox
The garden as place of contemplation 117
Time for change – petrol vs electricity in the garden . . 120
The garden in September – saving seeds 124
Awakening to Nature. 126

CONTENTS

October: Going Within
Autumn in the garden – reconnecting the inner
    with the outer 130
Do we need to 'get everything ready for Winter'?..... 135
Bulb planting in October 138
A happy accident? 140
The garden in October – towards Samhain 141

November: Fruitful Darkness
The garden in November........................ 144
Hedges – pruning, planting and making new
    friends? 147
Winter seed heads 150
Think before you dig 153

December: Midwinter Light
The Holly and the Ivy – Midwinter light 157
Leaves – Summer's gift, Winter's hope 160
The native hedge – a 'mini-woodland' in your
    garden 163
The Midwinter garden 165

Appendix: Eurythmy and Nature 169

Acknowledgements 171

About the Author 172

INTRODUCTION

In March of 2020, I was approached by the editor of our local newsletter "Forest Row Local", who asked if I would write a short monthly article on gardening. I agreed, and beginning with my first article in April "How Green is Your Grass? – Lawnmowing and Climate Change" I wrote 46 articles over the four-year period up to April 2024, which are now collected together in this book.

Forest Row is a Sussex village of around 7,000 residents, situated mid-way between London and Brighton in the beautiful Sussex Weald, where I have lived and worked for over 20 years. It is a very diverse village and those who live here hold many different views on life including opinions on gardening styles. These range from permaculture-inspired, 'no-digging' meadow enthusiasts who may have a relaxed attitude to tidiness, to 'traditional' lawn-loving horticulturalists who prefer things tidier. I myself am part of both of these traditions – I learnt gardening in the 1980's (at Writtle Agricultural College in Essex), where weedkillers, double-digging, lawn edging and tidiness were still very much taught and promoted; however, the world of gardening has moved on considerably since then, and whilst I too moved on towards a more 'relaxed' approach to nature, I still enjoy tidiness and cut lawns, at least in some parts of the garden. Thus, every month when I prepared the article, I felt the tension between the tidiness and the wildness that I experienced within myself reflected in the wider Forest Row community. For this I was grateful, because I could use the many and varied gardeners that I had come to know and love in the village as an imaginative audience to 'preview' my article, as a way to temper and celebrate both of these parts. Tidiness *is* important: 'permaculture' is not just about leaving the garden to grow exactly how it wishes, with a proliferation of weeds and unkempt areas everywhere; but *wildness* is important too – letting nature have her space and not controlling her too much. Many of my articles addressed this tension: the wild meadow versus the neat lawn, the pros and cons of rain, the native daffodil or the striking hybrid, cutting or leaving certain branches when pruning a tree, in essence the striving for harmony and balance in the garden.

Over the years, I returned again and again to these themes in my writing until today, when compiling the articles for this book, I realise that it is Nature herself who is driving this dialogue within me. It is she who is asking me to listen to her, to awaken to her. Nature has always embodied polarities: Winter/Summer, warm/cold, inbreathing/outbreathing, tidy/wild, living/dead, and whilst in the past we were intrinsically linked with these polarities in all aspects of our life, it was perhaps not very conscious. As an agrarian society, we all worked and lived with Nature, she surrounded us, and we simply accepted we were connected to her, often in a deeply spiritual way. We knew she was the 'Spirit of the Earth' and we celebrated and respected her. With the rise of industrialisation we began working at tasks often removed from Nature, and as we left the countryside for the town and city many of us may have forgotten her. But she is still here: all around us, above us, below us *and* within us; she is everywhere! I believe one of the important tasks of today is to find ways to awaken to Nature, to remember that 'I am at one with Nature', (as I always have been) but this time more consciously at one.

INTRODUCTION

There are many ways to consciously awaken to Nature: mindful walking, outdoor crafts and play, 'forest bathing', plant spirit journeys, guided meditations, sit spots/solo meditations, etc. but perhaps the simplest and oldest way is the humble art of gardening. Alongside becoming conscious of the polarities inherent in gardening and the striving for balance inwardly and outwardly (as described above), gardening is also intimately connected to the cycle of the year. Each season and each month have their own 'signature', their own quality, expressed through the weather (temperature, sunshine hours, rainfall etc) and also the day length; because of this, as a gardener, it is by default necessary to wake up. I need to know what season is coming next, will I be breathing in with the 'fruitful darkness' of Winter or breathing out to the 'worldwide life' of Summer, and how will our plants fare? I can't easily and successfully plant daffodils in May, and I can't really cut lawns in January. I need to acknowledge the seasons, the cycle of the year, but more than to just acknowledge I might also need to celebrate them. In the past, the seasons and major turning points of the year (the equinoxes, the solstices, and the mid-points between), lived within all of us as a reality and we celebrated them within and without. In the forgetfulness of today we might, however, need some help.

Two writers who are endlessly helpful and inspiring and whom I have often quoted in the following articles are Glennie Kindred and Rudolf Steiner. The first, Glennie Kindred, in her book 'The Earths Cycle of Celebration'[1] clearly and beautifully shares her wisdom on the eight Celtic

---

1 Glennie Kindred, "The Earth's Cycle of Celebration" (www.glenniekindred.co.uk)

festivals of Yule, Imbolc, The Spring Equinox, Beltane, Midsummer, Lammas, The Autumn Equinox and Samhain, and describes the inbreathing and outbreathing of the Spirit of the Earth and our relationship to this. Additionally, she is generous in sharing her knowledge about how this cycle of the year can be celebrated both inwardly and outwardly, and although her lovely book is not specifically about gardening in the normal sense of the word, it actually is. It describes the 'gardening' which we might want to practise to help us awaken to Nature: gardening as a sacred meditative art of both being and doing. Rudolf Steiner is the second author for whom I also have immense gratitude. Alongside his many and varied insights on biodynamic gardening, his beautiful and fascinating views about the Christian story and its relationship to the Spirit of the Earth, he also wrote the 'Soul Calendar'[2], a series of 52 meditative verses which offer us a way to inwardly connect to what we experience in outer nature throughout the year: the inbreathing and outbreathing described above.

The Celtic-based wisdom of Glennie Kindred and the Christian-based insights of Rudolf Steiner, do not, for me, present a problem of competing world views, because I experience them as both asking me to awaken to the Earth, her seasons and to love the Spirit of the Earth, namely Nature. The name of this love, whether it is called Celtic, Christian, Buddhist or other, is far less important than the free deed of loving in whatever way feels comfortable for us. I hope these articles will help and encourage the reader in this act of love, which necessarily involves bringing both inner meditative elements and outer practical activity to all

---

[2] Rudolf Steiner, "The Calendar of the Soul", (translated by Ruth and Hans Pusch, SteinerBooks Inc, United States).

that we do in our gardens. Additionally, I hope they may also encourage the reader to take these experiences and insights into the wider, existential relationship with Nature as an offering of connection, of awakening, of a loving co-creative act of healing for our times.

A NOTE ON CHRONOLOGY, NOUNS AND PRONOUNS

These articles were written over a four-year period, beginning in April 2020. They have been grouped together in the twelve months in which they were originally published but are not necessarily chronological. This is deliberate, because I wanted to let each month in the book 'breathe' in a way that balanced the practical with the meditative and some moving around felt necessary. In particular, I have placed the article which best introduces the mood of each month at the beginning of that chapter. To sense into the twelve moods of the gardening year most fully, I would recommend reading the book straight through from January to December, however, because each article was originally written as a stand-alone monthly gardening article, it can also be dipped into 'as and when'.

There are times when one article (written in February 2023, say) refers to an earlier article (written in April 2021). Because I have grouped the chapters together month by month, there a few instances of the 'future' being described before the 'past', and in the spirit of keeping the articles 'true' to the month they were written I haven't changed them, instead giving a reference to the upcoming article. I hope this occasional exercise in 'time-travel' does not detract or confuse too much, particularly as the articles were, as mentioned above, written to be read as single articles.

Throughout the book I have capitalised the word 'Nature', as well as the four seasons, the twelve months, and all the festivals. This is intentional, as for me, it raises them to the status of proper nouns, which I believe they are. By consciously acknowledging this status, I hope it helps the reader to feel into the new relationship with Nature which I want to suggest in this book: one where humans and nature are equal partners; each of us with our true and 'proper' name. When using a pronoun to refer to a plant or to some aspect of Nature, I have chosen not to use the word 'it' as I feel this is an unhelpful and old-fashioned way of objectifying a living being. However, I have not been consistent in my use of pronouns, mostly using 'she' but sometimes using 'they'; the choice of each pronoun has arisen in each instance spontaneously as a response to my personal feeling when interacting meditatively with a particular plant/element of Nature and is a work in progress.

A GARDENING WHEEL OF THE YEAR

The wheel that I have drawn overleaf is a very simple interpretation of the cycle of the year, based on my subjective experiences as both a gardener for 45 years and someone who has lived into the ideas of the inbreathing and outbreathing of the Earth as described in this book. For me, drawing my inner experiences is a good way to free them from my intellect, connect to my feeling sense, which then often allows me to look in unusual directions. This might be of help to others as well.

This should not be taken as a definitive guide, but rather as a pointer where each image can act as an imaginative seed in the mind of the reader. I hope these simple pictures can be used as meditative reference points whilst the book is being read to help connect with the underlying life-force of each month as it changes and flows throughout the Wheel of the Year.

Whilst the wheel can be read as portraying gardening tasks and activities that take place in any *single* month – apple harvesting, composting, etc. I would suggest that another way is to look at *pairs* of months, specifically those diametrically opposite each other. Here we might more easily feel into the sense of inbreathing and outbreathing of the Earth, the balance and change points within that cycle, as well as some simple polarities of light and dark, life and death, movement and stillness.

January and July: the cycle of composting. Compost made in **July** (outbreathing) is spread under fruit trees in **January** (inbreathing).

February and August: seed and fruit. The first stirrings of growth beginning in **February** reach a certain culmination in **August** with the first fruits.

March and September: the Equinoxes as points of balance and change. The Earth begins her great outbreath in **March** and commences drawing herself in again in **September.**

April and October: the polarities described above continue in these two months – **April** is full of life and growth upwards, whilst **October** is a letting go downwards.

May and November: nearing culmination! Lush and strong meadows in **May,** beautiful and fragile seed heads in **November.**

June and December: Midsummer and Midwinter moods. The Earth, Nature and all her beings have done their work – a time for a pause, a standing still. Living with the outer Sun in **June**, living with the inner Sun in **December.**

A GARDENING WHEEL OF THE YEAR

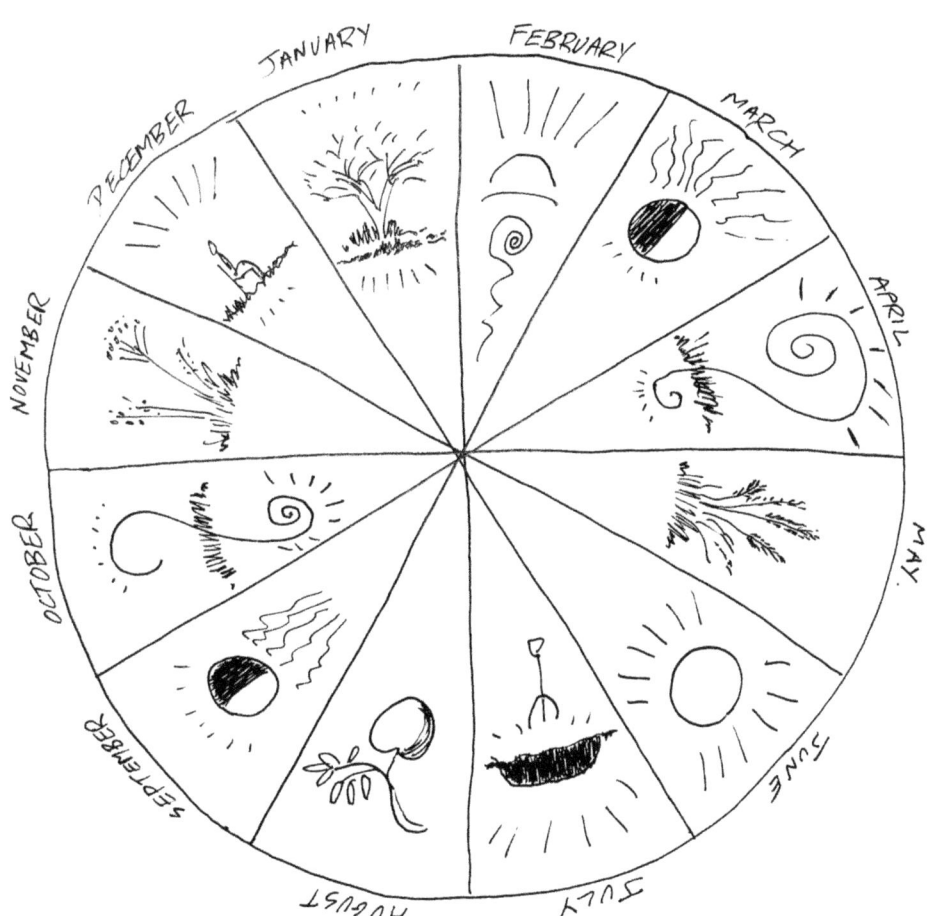

JANUARY
Beginnings

Wonderful witch hazel, New Year experiments and the forgotten art of 'conscious compromise' when pruning fruit trees.

WITCH HAZEL – JANUARY'S WINTER BLOOM

If I was asked to choose just only one shrub to have in my garden, it might well be the witch hazel which is beginning to blossom now in January. The plant, with her delicate flowers of yellow, orange or red brings welcome cheer to the Winter days: the lightly-scented petals themselves are quite subtle (resembling grated cheese), but they hold themselves in profusion on bare stems and, set against a blue Winter sky, can be striking. Add a covering of snow or frost and the combination of colours and textures in the sharp, clear light of January can be stunning. In these early days of the New Year, when we are emerging from the cocoon of the Midwinter Holy Nights and it seems the days are just deciding whether to lengthen or not, the witch hazel can give us hope that Spring will indeed come.

Witch hazels are deciduous shrubs that can grow up to fifteen feet high, and whose Latin name *Hamamelis* means 'together with the fruit,' referring to the simultaneous occurrence of the flowers with the maturing fruit of last year. Originally from North America, the plant was used by indigenous cultures for dowsing, and thus leads us to its English name – witch hazel, coming from the Middle English 'wicke' for 'lively' and 'wych', an Anglo-Saxon word for 'bend' – both words describing the action of a dowsing rod which can bend towards the ground when water is detected below. The plant has many medicinal properties, particularly for skin problems, including rashes, sunburn and minor cuts, additionally branches hung in a house are said to offer protection; witch hazel is thus an important part of a Nature healer's range of remedies, and gives us a further clue to its name.

So, it's a magical, healing and protective plant, beautiful and hope-inducing now in Winter, but why else would I choose it as a favourite? Well, it is also very attractive in Spring – the fresh green leaves appearing on the pleasing framework of stems are a very heartening sight, and in my garden these stems provide a great perch for robins and sparrows visiting the nearby pond, queuing to bathe in the waters below. Later, at the end of the season in Autumn, the leaves can turn through the most exquisite range of colours – golds, reds, greens and browns, sometimes all at the same time on the same leaf, providing many weeks of amazing table decorations to honour the passing of the Summer. Coupled with the fact that the shrub is slow-growing and compact, requires minimal pruning, is not affected by frost or drought and suffers rarely from pests and diseases, the witch hazel is hard to beat for its year-round value and should, in my view, have a place in every garden.

(January 2023)

THE GARDEN IN JANUARY

January is a time to look forward to the New Year and all that it may bring, both outwardly and inwardly. So, what is happening outwardly in the garden now and what inner resolutions could I bring to it?

The days are just starting to lengthen and there is often a particularly hopeful feeling in the air, even if sometimes the weather can be challenging for many more weeks. The fruit trees are awaiting care, as is the wisteria (for fruit tree pruning, see below). For wisterias that have reached their allotted space, then it is simply the case of pruning the flowering stems back to two or three strong buds (these would have already been pruned in the Summer, back to around six inches). By pruning hard, the flowering potential is concentrated into these few buds, maximising the effect. If the wisteria is still young, then the trailing shoots can be positioned to where you want the mature plant to be, ideally tied onto a strong framework of vine eyes and wires. Other jobs in January might be spreading compost on dormant beds (followed by turning the newer compost), as well as feeding fruit trees by strewing a fine layer of compost under the whole crown of the tree, not just up close to the stem. The reason for the large area of application is that the fine roots which take in nutrients are at the very edge of the root system, which mostly mirrors the size of the crown. It may look a little untidy for a few weeks, but soon the compost will be taken down to the roots by rain and worm activity. Finally, my favourite Winter job when the weather is challenging: cleaning and tidying greenhouses and tool sheds. Within the shed, tools can be cleaned with water and a scrubbing brush, and then the metal treated with vegetable oil and the wood with linseed oil.

My Three New Year Experiments

In the spirit of New Year's resolutions, I am trying three garden experiments – things I don't usually do, but will try out.

A) Prune buddleia in March. Most horticultural guides suggest that these shrubs should be pruned in Autumn, but this year I will prune mine as late as possible – ideally just before growth starts in March. I am hoping that not only will I (and wildlife) enjoy the gently decaying foliage and seed heads throughout the Winter, but that it will also encourage the plant to flower later in the year. The aim is that this will most benefit butterflies, who love the buddleia flowers, and who are most prolific in the later part of the Summer.

B) Leave some leaves. This is difficult for me – despite my wish to leave some areas of wildness in my garden, leaves seem to be always tidied away. I will try to leave some leaves on my lawns – not too many that they smother and kill the grass or meadow, but enough to provide a place for insects and worms, both to benefit the soil and also to provide a Winter food source for birds.

JANUARY

C) Stop digging soil circles around trees. I have always been taught that a tree in a lawn/meadow should have a circle of soil around it to help it 'breathe', to take in nutrients and to prevent competition with grass and wildflowers. Whilst this could be the case for newly planted trees, I am realising that mature trees might not need this. Trees 'breathe' through their leaves and stems which are above the soil and take in nutrients through their fine root systems which, as explained above, are not near the trunk, but rather at the very edge of the tree crown. With regards to competition, the new soil science suggests that plants actually like living with each other – often the root system of one benefits another, through the exchange of nutrients. This could mean that removing plants from around the trunk of a tree may be unhelpful. I do not know this for sure, but it seems worth an experiment!

(January 2022)

WINTER PRUNING OF APPLE AND PEAR TREES

Now that the busy days of Autumn tidying are behind us, the month of January is a good time for Winter pruning of fruit trees. Without their leaves, the trees in their stark beauty allow us a chance to look closely at their structural form and prune accordingly. This article will concentrate on apple and pear pruning, as all stone fruits (plums, cherries and gages) should not be pruned in Winter as they are susceptible to 'silverleaf' – a serious fungal disease transmitted through moisture in pruning cuts.

Fruit trees, like all plants, have a desire to propagate themselves and if left unchecked will try to produce as many fruits as possible. In the case of an apple tree, for example, they will try to revert to a wild crab apple – many dense branches bearing sometimes hundreds of small fruits. As gardeners, we are trying to find a way to balance the wish of the tree for propagation and self-perpetuation with our wishes for good quality fruit, tree health and aesthetic enjoyment – an inevitable compromise will have to be reached, personal to each of us and our understanding of what a tree is for. There are three basic rules to pruning of apples and pears, under the headings 1) light and air, 2) size, and 3) renewal of fruiting wood. If we follow these rules then we have gone a long way to helping the tree reach the balance suggested above; further detailed, smaller scale pruning is still possible but is outside the scope of this article.

1) Light and air. To increase the health of a garden tree compared to their wild counterpart, it is helpful to allow more light, and air, into their crown. Both light and air are vital to the health of trees and their fruits: a very dense, unpruned tree will have many twiggy dead branches and often the fruits will not ripen well; one senses a kind of 'matted stagnation' in the crown, a feeling of 'stuck' air flow and loss of light. To obviate this, we can remove a number of large crossing, old, or dying branches using a good pruning saw. Try to look at the tree from a distance and prune those branches which will not only create a more open framework, but with their removal might also make the shape of the tree more aesthetically pleasing. Cut decisively and generously, choose thicker branches over thinner and don't leave short stumps which will die back, but rather cut as close to the stem as possible (NB: it is important to cut above the branch bark ridge which is a raised, angled ridge visible at all branch junctions and is needed to help healing of the cut). As a general rule, prune out a maximum of an eighth of internal branches in any one year: more in a very neglected tree, less in a well-pruned one. Once we have finished with the saw, there may be other smaller branches requiring removal with secateurs. Again, crossing, old or dying branches should be chosen.

2) Size. The ultimate size of a fruit tree is dependent upon its root stock, so it is important to choose the correct root stock when purchasing a tree; a good nursery or garden centre will help with this. For those of us who have inherited large trees which feel too big for our garden, we will have to make compromises. If the tree has a very vigorous root stock then no matter how much we prune them for size, they will always re-grow to their 'pre-planned' size; we will either have to live with, remove or manage them. Managing the size means reducing the longest branches every year by a few feet, which will not only reduce the tree's size but will also encourage side shoots and fruit growth on the branch. However, do not expect a miracle in size reduction: if we try to cut the tree too hard, we will be rewarded the following year with a mass of incredibly strong, vigorous growths – sometimes longer than the ones we removed the previous year! We must remember they are, and want to be, a large tree.

3) Renewal of fruiting wood. On all fruit trees there are two types of bud – fruit buds and leaf buds. Fruit buds are identifiable as being thicker, rougher, plumper and older than the smoother, smaller younger leaf buds. If one observes a single branch of a fruit tree, the leaf buds are the first buds at the very tip of a branch: they are small, smooth and close to the stem. If we look further down the stem to the second and third year of growth, we can see these buds have now transformed into fruit buds – thicker and more upright, perhaps in a cluster or spur. A healthy fruit tree needs constant renewal of both sorts of buds and a good balance of the two: young and old wood. Most of this renewal comes about naturally if we carry out the above two rules correctly because 1) removal of old wood for light and air allows young wood to develop, and 2) reduction of size by removing the tips of branches encourages development of fruit buds and spurs lower down (NB: there are a few varieties of apple which have some fruit buds on the tips of their branches (for example Worcester Pearmain, Lord Lambourne and Pink Lady – here we will have to be more judicious in our pruning: it will be crucial to identify the fruit buds and not cut them off! In practice this means less size reduction). A further simple pruning technique to bring about this balance is to reduce young side shoots on main branches by three or four buds – this helps concentrate energy on the fruit buds and spurs lower down rather than on too much leafy growth.

A final thought. Before pruning, it is a good idea to stand back and really look at the tree. All trees are unique and have their own character and being. By really observing, we start to form a connection, a dialogue with the tree; we begin to notice particular branches, fruits and the way that they are growing. Many indigenous cultures, including

JANUARY

Britain's own Celtic/Druidic stream, develop this theme further – they suggest we should gently ask the tree for permission before cutting and also ask for guidance on how to prune: an almost forgotten art, but one which deserves reviving. It does require a shift in our gardener's mindset of being the one in charge and needs a few moments of reflection before action, but it can be really helpful. For me, this 'getting to know' a tree is the first stage of pruning, if we are quiet enough, we may well be guided to the right way to prune them: it might be different from what we first imagined, and it might also be very different from a neighbouring tree. By practicing this attitude each time we prune, we might come closer to the balance outlined at the beginning – the compromise between the wishes of the tree and our wishes. This quality of 'conscious compromise' could also inform our wider relationships to the other non-human beings of the Earth – other plants, plus minerals and the animals – and lead to healing of the damage which we have carried out on the Earth in the name of 'human-first' growth, replacing it with a kinder, more thoughtful and more reciprocal way of relating.

(January 2021)

FEBRUARY
The Light Returns

Imbolc and Candlemas, the Lent Lily, Winter rain and the balance of intellect with intuition.

THE GARDEN IN FEBRUARY – 'THE LIGHT RETURNS'

As we move into the month of February, with its often bitter and cold weather, gardeners might ask the questions: will Winter ever end? Will our gardens ever be green again? Will it ever change, or will it stay dark forever? However, if we look closely at Nature, the signs of awakening are all around: tree buds are beginning to thicken, snowdrops and crocuses are now flowering, as well as many early blossoming shrubs like witch hazel, Winter honeysuckle, daphne and camellias; additionally, since the

New Year we can notice the lengthening of the days and the welcoming quality of this increased light. This twofold experience – a feeling of gloom and questioning set against the coming of light and growth – is a key to understanding this moment in the gardening year and has been celebrated for centuries in different spiritual traditions. In the Celtic tradition, the beginning of February is known as Imbolc or St. Bride's Day, whilst Christian tradition uses the term 'Candlemas'. Essentially, they are celebrating the same thing: the return of the light and the powers of growth; and often the rituals connected to these festivals involve the lighting of candles on or in the earth, a symbolic celebration of the mystery of the germination of the seed, and the fertile power of the Spirit of the Earth. Glennie Kindred writes in her book, *The Earths Cycle of Celebration*:

> *"Imbolc is a celebration of the life force. [...] Here we can use the inner wisdom we have gained during the Winter months and bring it out into the active part of the year. The spark of intuition and the intellect of consciousness join together to bring about fertility and growth on all levels. This union of the two aspects of ourselves creates a magical and fertile time, a time of awakenings and new beginnings, charged with the potency of rising energy [...]. Our acceptance of Winter is giving way to an urge to move forward into Springtime energy."*

What can we do as gardeners in this time to find a connection to all this? In February, formative pruning of fruit trees, shrubs and climbers can continue. By pruning, we acknowledge the transition from inner to outer and trust that by cutting and removing wood, we are also initiating new growth. Wisteria can be cut back to two or three strong buds and any young growth either removed or trained – this will help the plant to have larger, stronger flower trusses in May. Clematis, apart from the shrubby Montana variety, can now be cut back hard – again a confidence in the mysterious inner power of re-growth. Dogwoods can be pruned now, the simplest way is to cut the whole plant down to the ground – they will regrow and they will soon reward us with their wonderful flame-coloured young stems. Fruit tree pruning (as discussed in my previous article) embodies the same process. Roses are the exception to this rule, as they flower on soft young growth; if we prune them too early then the young shoots may well become frosted and flowering will be affected – pruning is best held off until March.

Another beneficial activity that can be carried out now is compost spreading. The compost which we collected in the previous Summer is now ready for use and can be spread around the garden. This has a threefold purpose – firstly, we empty the compost area ready for the new season; secondly, we bring much needed fertility for the soil; and thirdly, it can help us form an imaginative connection to the quotation above – Summer's growth is transformed through the "inner wisdom" of Winter composting, helping to bring about the Spring awakening. The vegetable patch is an obvious candidate for compost, but it can also be put on flower beds as a mulch, both conditioning and feeding the soil as well as inhibiting weeds. Additionally, spreading it around the bases of roses and shrubs, as well as fruit trees, is also really beneficial. When mulching fruit trees, remember to spread the compost lightly under the whole crown of the tree, not just close to the stem – because the smallest and most active roots of the tree are the ones furthest away from the trunk. Although it may look a little untidy for a few weeks, it will quite soon be taken down to the roots by both rain and earthworm activity and by the time of the first lawn cut it will have disappeared.

A third way to connect to this time of year is to order seeds – the archetypal 'new beginning'. When choosing seeds, as well as making the usual choices of flavour, pest-resilience and reliability (in the case of vegetables), and longevity and flowering ability (in the case of annual flowers), there are some other aspects to be aware of. Many seeds sold today are paradoxically not particularly garden-friendly, so look out for the following on the packet: 1) organic/biodynamic (grown in harmony with Nature, without the use of poisonous herbicides and pesticides); 2) open-pollinated (insect-pollinated plants that produce nectar for bees, have built-in genetic diversity and can be saved for resowing). Thankfully there are a few companies in the UK that supply seeds that are both reliable and pest-resistant as well as being organic and open-pollinated (although Tamar Seeds and the Organic Gardening Catalogue also sell non-open-pollinated 'F1 hybrids', which should be avoided).

A final thought – as mentioned earlier, the weather in February can be very inclement, so alongside dressing warmly and being adequately prepared for all the elements, we can also prepare ourselves inwardly by aligning ourselves to the wisdom of those who have perceived the inner Nature of this time. Rudolf Steiner's *Soul Calendar* helps us here and the verse for the end of January can bring a further poetic, meditative layer of connection (and inner protection?) and a glimpse into the hopeful Spring that will soon come!

"In this, the shrouding gloom of Winter
The soul feels ardently impelled
To manifest its innate strength,
To guide it into darknesses,
Anticipating thus, through warmth of heart,
The sense-world's revelation."

(Soul Calendar – 3rd week of January)

(February 2021)

OUR NATIVE DAFFODIL – THE LENT LILY

"I never saw daffodils so beautiful; they lie among the mossy stones about them, some rested their heads upon these stones as on a pillow for weariness and the rest tossed and reeled and danced and seemed as if they verily laughed with the wind that blew upon them over the lake; they looked so gay, ever dancing, ever changing."

– Dorothy Wordsworth.

As a professional gardener for over 40 years, my views on plants and planting styles have evolved over time; this is particularly true in my relation to the daffodil. When I started out in the parks departments of Southampton and Perth in Scotland, I was an avid fan of hybrid daffodils, designing them into any planting plan I could: flower beds, meadows and even roundabouts. I liked the fresh vibrancy of them, the instant brightness, the spectacular colours and forms: small, medium, large, single, semi-double, double, scented, frilled, multi-coloured, multi-stemmed, and so on. There is no denying that they can be spectacular in the right setting and, flowering usually around Easter, they can bring a wonderful sense of relief that Winter is over and that the forces of life and resurrection are present all around us. I think this is why I felt so attracted to them and why we collectively still plant so many in our gardens.

However, over the years my tastes have changed, and I feel less attracted to the garishness of the hybrid daffodils and feel more drawn to the original native daffodil – *Daffodil pseudonarcissus* – from which all the other hybrids have been developed. The daffodil itself is small, around 15–20cm in height, with a simple yellow single trumpet and slim green leaves. That's it! Barely any scent, no frills, no other colours. Not spectacular, not outstanding, rather humble. However, their humility works well when they are harmoniously growing *en masse* – in my opinion, the best way to enjoy these daffodils. The most famous places to view these plants are not only in the Lake District (at Ullswater, for example – made famous by Dorothy and William Wordsworth), but also in Farndale in the North Yorkshire Moors, and the 'golden triangle' of Gloucestershire around the villages of Dymock and Kempley. Additionally, closer to home, there are areas in the Ashdown Forest (around Pooh Bridge and along the banks of Tabell Ghyll) where one can also see them.

If you are not able to visit these places then it is possible to replicate the effect in your own gardens: planting in large drifts in areas of meadow. I don't recommend planting daffodils in flower beds as they tend to look ugly after flowering as the leaves have to remain (and wither) for up to 10 weeks after flowering. If this doesn't happen, the bulb will be blind the following year as it has not received enough nutrition through the photosynthesising leaves. In meadows, this is of course not a problem as the leaves become assimilated and then lost into the general Summer growth of the other meadow plants. When planting, buy as many as you can afford and be generous and not too ambitious: choose a few patches with many bulbs (say, at least 30-40 in small gardens, more in larger gardens) rather than many patches with only a few in number – this will replicate the 'drift' effect seen in Nature. Additionally, don't try to position the bulbs too carefully – follow the advice of William Robinson, the famous gardener of the last century (and designer of nearby Gravetye Manor Garden), who advocated throwing the bulbs on the ground and planting them where they landed – sometimes close to each other, sometimes further away. Both these techniques will help replicate the natural look.

On a final point – there are now real dangers that the above-mentioned areas of wild daffodils are being threatened by hybrid daffodils, simply by the large numbers of the latter now being planted and cross-pollinating with the wild ones. There are conservationists in these areas warning of this threat, both horticulturally and aesthetically, suggesting that one way we could help is to plant less hybrids and more of the native daffodil (in 2010, one conservationist, Dr Andy Tasker, the former chief executive of the Warwickshire Wildlife Trust, launched a one-man campaign against the practice, describing efforts to brighten up road verges and picnic spots with modern strains of daffodils *"like painting lipstick on the Mona Lisa"*).

Whilst we don't need to be too fundamental in our aesthetic choices – sometimes 'bling' in the garden can be fun and welcome, I believe that a move towards the humbler native plants and styles like wild daffodils in drifts may help counteract the 'busy-ness' of life. Perhaps we sometimes need to let go of our of need for ever more excitement and find a way back to natural planting styles, reminding us that Nature is nourishing in her natural humility. It is interesting that the wild daffodil is also known as the 'Lent Lily', flowering as it does in the period leading up to Easter – traditionally a time to be frugal and humble. Maybe by planting more of these simple, 'quiet' Spring flowers we can feel into the Lenten mood a bit deeper, sensing the truth of William Wordsworth's observation: *"With an eye made quiet by the power of harmony and the deep power of joy, we see into the life of things."*

(February 2022)

RAIN IN THE GARDEN

"Water is the driving force in Nature."

– Leonardo da Vinci.

As I write this, in the middle of January, I have woken up to another day of torrential rain, and I ask myself: 'is all this rain a good or bad thing for the garden?' Reflecting on this, my answer is 'probably both'. Below are my thoughts on this.

Excessive rain is undoubtedly detrimental to some plants: heavy rain can break plant stems and if the soil is too wet then certain plants will simply rot, particularly those which love dry, well-drained soil. For example, lavender, artemisia, lamb's ears and dianthus have little tolerance for wet soil and can die after just a day or two of sogginess (this could happen even if I add gravel around the plant to help with drainage). There are no easy remedies to this problem – a move to a choice of plants more tolerant of wet conditions could be one solution: three common examples are lily-of the valley, forget-me-not and the red Siberian dogwood. Another problem is that trees may start to lean – caused by rotting/soggy roots, excessive water on the leaves plus accompanying high winds – in the short-term, staking a leaning tree is a solution; in the longer term, particularly if the tree is large and poses a risk, expert advice from a tree surgeon should be sought.

A lot of rain in the garden is also a challenge to the gardener. Much rain gear is required – waterproof clothing plus boots, gloves, hats and often scarves. Mobility and subtle awareness can be greatly impaired – being able to listen and see all around, particularly to birds, is for me an enjoyable and important part of gardening. I often receive helpful thoughts from listening and feeling meditatively into the plants and animals present in the garden, which is challenging when closed-off against the weather. And even when I get out in the garden, fully protected against the elements, there are some areas where I just cannot work in heavy rain – flower and vegetable beds and parts of lawns and meadows that don't fully drain – working here will compact the soil too much, leading to loss of soil structure, reduced aeration, reduced microbial activity, and hence reduced life. The only solution to this is to get off the soil and wait for drier days.

However, there are positive aspects too. Remembering last Summer – endless days of blue skies and record-breaking temperatures; although on many levels wonderful, water levels in many reservoirs became very low as the drought began to bite, leading eventually to a hosepipe ban and plants often dying. Clearly the season of heavy rain now will help fill the reservoirs, and also any rainwater collection systems in our gardens.

Secondly, if I realise that for a good part of the Winter, I may not be able to work on flower and vegetable beds due to excessive moisture, then maybe I should change my maintenance ideas? Maybe I need to design flower beds and meadow and lawns that don't need much Winter work? This could mean increasing ground cover plants below shrubs and thickly mulching beds in Autumn with compost – both techniques will reduce annual weeds and will reduce the need to weed in the Winter. Additionally, ground cover and mulching will help prevent excessive loss of topsoil – something that is a real danger with heavy rain on bare soil. Unfortunately, pruning is harder to time well – cutting herbaceous plants in early Autumn saves them from soil compaction and rain damage in the Winter, but the cost to this is that there is less dead material for birds, insects and also for displaying Winter frost. Choosing the 'right' moment to prune is therefore an ongoing question for me…

Thirdly, and perhaps the most subtle, is that I might need to change my attitude to rain. Wet weather is often referred to as 'bad' and dry weather as 'good', but I wonder if this is helpful? Humans are 70% water, and this element, as Leonardo da Vinci understood, is the most important carrier of life forces in us and in Nature. Without water, we would soon die – so maybe experiencing rain, lots of it, is a wake-up call for me to change my attitude to 'bad weather', embrace the rain and find an inner meditative connection to it. I have written before about eurythmy (see *"Movement is Life"* – August 2021), the movement art developed by Rudolf Steiner, and in recent years there have been some inspiring eurythmy gestures and sequences developed that do just this. One of these sequences involves creating a generous circle or lemniscate (figure of eight) with my arms above and around my body, moving this in a gentle, flowing, and repetitive way and accompanying it with simple spoken phrases. With the guidance of a professional eurythmist (essential at the beginning), this exercise has helped me find an inner meditative connection to water, a connection that transcends good and bad, and leads to an acceptance of both in a flowing and open way (see Appendix 1 – *Eurythmy and Nature*).

To end, here is an inspiring excerpt from the poem, *A Rainy Day*, by the Albanian poet, Visar Ziti, beautifully encapsulating a new attitude that may need to arise within us if we are not to feel overwhelmed by 'all this rain'…

"It rains,
And rains,
And rains.
But there is a sky above the rain,
Nothing can rot the sky.
Earth has turned to mud. What of it?
The heart of the planet is made of fire, of ardent sun."

(February 2023)

FEBRUARY

THE UNION OF INTUITION WITH INTELLECT

As I write this article, in mid-January, the days are slowly increasing in length, the birds are becoming more active, and the first signs of bulbs, especially snowdrops, are seen. Although the weather at this time can be challenging, my feeling is one of hopeful optimism as I try to accompany inwardly the sense of rebirth that I see all around me. At the beginning of February, this awakening process is celebrated in the festivals of Candlemas and Imbolc, and although I have already quoted Glennie Kindred's suggestions on the mood of this time, I want to repeat part of it below as it is both simple, beautiful and very helpful.

> "Imbolc is a celebration of the life force. [...] Here we can use the inner wisdom we have gained during the Winter months and bring it out into the active part of the year. The spark of intuition and the intellect of consciousness join together to bring about fertility and growth on all levels."

Kindred is asking us to connect to the marriage of the female and male within each of us and their respective expressions of intuition and intellect – and garden work in January and February, to my mind, neatly reflects this mood. There are many plants that need pruning now – fruit trees, climbing roses and wisteria to name three. Each need slightly different pruning, but essentially it is a recognition that some of the old needs to be cut away to encourage new growth. The pruning does indeed need a marriage of instinct and intellect as mentioned in the above quote: not only the obvious dead and old wood needs to be cut away, but also attention needs to be paid to how the plant looks, and how it wants to look for the coming year.

With fruit trees, my January article has given the details – these are essentially: 1) remove dead, diseased, dying and crossing branches; 2) thin out overcrowded clumps of branches; 3) encourage fruit spurs by cutting back long new growths by about a third; and 4) trust your intuition in asking the tree how it would like to look in the coming year and modify your pruning accordingly, for example leaving older unproductive branches that have a pleasing form. Climbing roses also need a degree of balance between intellect and intuition – older, dead and dying stems should be removed, and younger shoots should be tied in; whilst at the same time the overall form of the rose should still look pleasing. This is achieved through careful tying-in of new stems in such a way that there is good space between each: I often try to make a fan of equally spaced branches raying out from the base and, if necessary, moving the older stems to accommodate this. Wisteria, which had their Summer prune in July, now needs a further cutting back to two buds on every spur. Even this is not straightforward, and a degree of intuition is again required: sometimes more than two buds should be left if the plant is a little thin in a certain place, and sometimes more should be cut if the plant is growing too wide.

Vegetable Garden Update

This time last year (see *April 2023: A Simple Vegetable Garden*), the garden I wrote about was only a wish, and was in fact only lawn. In March, I laid out the basic plan and set about building it according to the 'no-dig' principles of

FEBRUARY

Charles Dowding: lots of cardboard covered with compost, leaf mould and wood chips (for the paths) placed directly on top of the lawn. I have to say that I have been very impressed with the results: firstly, much to my surprise, the lawn did indeed fade away under the cardboard and mulch; secondly, the vegetables all did very well; and thirdly, the weed problem was minimal. Now, at the end of the year, I have restocked the mulch, the compost and the wood chips. This year everything (except a fine layer of wood chips to top the paths) has been provided from within the garden: six-month-old compost comprising kitchen waste, benign weeds and grass clippings, two year old leaf mould from nearby trees and green wood chippings from some tree work carried out within the garden. Looking at the results at the turn of the year is a satisfying experience, remembering the development of this space and now looking forward to another year. One change I will make is to put a deep wooden board at the back of the bed to hold the soil as this area tended to 'slip' and get mixed up with the neighbouring flower bed.

(February 2024)

MARCH

The Time of Balance and Awakening

Remembering the wisdom of the past, the art of making mistakes, rose pruning and eco-heaps.

THE SPRING EQUINOX – THE FESTIVAL OF BALANCE AND AWAKENING

Whilst writing this article in mid-February, the feeling in the garden was eerily quiet. All the fruit trees had been pruned and composted, beds weeded and mulched, the compost turned. The yellowing montbretia leaves still brought joy as did the numerous dried seed heads on the St. John's wort, fennel and purple loosestrife. There was some movement in the garden with the first stirrings of snowdrops and crocuses, but overall, it was quiet. Even though the days were increasing, time seemed to stand still. Now, however, just a few weeks later as we edge towards the Spring Equinox on the 21st of March and the festival of Easter, time is speeding up. Glennie Kindred in her book, *The Earth's Cycle of Celebration*, talks of the Equinox as …

> "… the first day of Spring. The balance of day and night, light and dark, inner and outer, intuitive and rational, conscious and unconscious, female and male. Plans which have been incubating on the inner levels since the Autumn Equinox can now hatch out onto the physical plane. The egg is a potent symbol here, full of potential and new life. A time to celebrate the fertile goddess Oestre (the root of the word Oestrogen, the hormone stimulating ovulation), the union of the male and female within ourselves regardless of gender".

I experience this time of year as one of great joy, but also a time of a little panic – everything is happening at once! The buddleias and remaining herbaceous plants must now be finally trimmed, the grass needs its first light cut, the roses need pruning, weeds start growing, seeds need sowing: everything in Nature is coming alive. Over the years, I have realised that gardening is like a series of dances – sometimes slow, sometimes fast, but each one needing to be at the right speed to suit the outer conditions in Nature. In the far distant past, we all instinctively knew how to dance these dances. We lived so closely with Nature that we felt we were part of her: when the thunder roared, we felt we were the thunder, when the river sang ,we were the river, when the plants began growing we felt a deep kinship with their growth. We were not separate: the dances came quite naturally to all of us; we instinctively knew when and how to work with the plants and animals around us.

Today, most of us have lost this instinctive knowledge. We have become educated, able to understand the technical elements of the world, but have sacrificed this all-knowing, this feeling of at-one-ness. I think this is why I am sometimes agitated around the Equinox – will I remember how to dance with Nature this year? Will I find the right tempo? Not too slow, but also not too fast. It doesn't come naturally anymore, at least not for me.

Help, however, is at hand. All the spiritual streams that have survived in the world have had Nature as their core. Sometimes this has become hidden, perhaps particularly in the case of Christianity, but nevertheless the earth is intrinsic to the meaning of Christianity and if one looks deep enough one discovers that the Christian festivals are all linked to the in-breath and out-breath in Nature, to the cycle of the year. The Celtic wisdom as expressed by Glennie Kindred in the quotation above shows that this stream also never lost sight of the earth and her changes. I believe we owe deep gratitude to these and many other indigenous streams who have kept the knowledge of the cycle of the year alive, who remind us that the earth is a living, breathing organism and we are part of that organism, dancing along with the changes.

So, as we enter another gardening season, I will try to remember some of the wisdom from the spiritual streams that have their roots in the far past and use their signposts – the festivals, to help me find my relationship to Nature. In particular, I will try to remember how to dance with her in my gardening – not too slow, not too fast. Rudolf Steiner, the founder of biodynamic agriculture, in his *Soul Calendar* wrote 52 weekly poetic signposts to meditate upon over the life of the year: in effect 52 mini-festivals. These signposts are not only meant to feed our soul, but are also supposed to spur us into action, in our working and connecting with the in-breathing and out-breathing in Nature. By offering us an inner soul pointer, in Steiner's words "a vigorous finding of oneself" in "feeling unison with the world's course" we can find clues in how to dance with Nature throughout the year; whether it is through practical gardening or by simply spending time in Nature. His verse for Spring is an inspiring call for us to awaken into the world's soul-spirit reality:

"When out of world-wide spaces
The sun speaks to the human mind,
And gladness from the depths of soul
Becomes, in seeing, one with light,
Then rising from the sheath of self,
Thought soar to distances of space
And dimly bind
The human being to the spirit's life."

(Soul Calendar – 2nd week of April)

(March 2022)

THE ART OF 'INCORRECT' GARDENING

"Learn the rules like a pro, so you can break them like an artist."

– Pablo Picasso.

Over my years as a gardener, I have built up a long list of rules for 'correct' gardening that I proudly preach to anyone who will listen, and which seem to be cast in stone. In the spirit of the quote above by the artist Picasso, here are some activities which are 'not allowed' in gardening but which upon reflection might just be ok; all of which I have personally done already this year!

Using the lawnmower in February. I used to say that it was 'against my religion' to cut grass in January and February, but I have just done this in a meadow in one of my gardens. Admittedly, it was a very special situation because it was going to be grazed over the Winter by sheep who in the end never arrived. The meadow was looking very shaggy and the first bulbs were about to come through: I decided that by mowing it on a high cut it would remove the bulk of the shagginess whilst probably not damaging too many bulb tips. I have to admit that it does look smart and ready to show off the crocuses and daffodils, so it feels like a good decision.

Putting weeds on the leaf pile because the compost heap is too full. The leaf pile is supposed to be for leaves, so therefore nothing else should be allowed to go on it. Whilst this is technically true, I think it is ok now and again to add other organic matter. This is because leaves need two years to rot and therefore a small amount of other material will definitely decompose well within that timeframe. However, the usual rule of no 'bad weeds' (ground elder, bindweed, and seeded docks) should never be ignored.

Putting leaves on the compost heap because the leaf pile is too far away. Surely this is 'not allowed'? Based on the above logic, the leaves will not rot in time (compost needing only a 6-month cycle). However, as long as it doesn't become a lazy habit, I would suggest it is occasionally alright to do this, particularly if the compost is very wet and therefore in danger of stagnation – because the leaves will add some dryness and form to encourage air into the heap and aid the composting process.

Leaving herbaceous plants in a flower bed about to be accessed by builders. I recently made this decision with some beautiful purple hellebores which were in their full prime. I was very tempted to move them out of the way of the imminent builders but was persuaded to leave them because a) the builders might actually see them, appreciate them and therefore give them a wide berth and b) moving the plants would disturb their still developing root system, arguably more important than the loss of flowers. So, I will observe what happens and hope that any pruning of stems and flowers by feet above ground will only serve to strengthen the root system which should continue to develop below the ground, unseen and hopefully undamaged.

So, as the gardening season begins in earnest in March, maybe we could break some of our rules and do something 'incorrect' – in the process we might learn something new and useful. Perhaps the advice of the famous scientist Albert Einstein is all we need to begin:

> "Anyone who has never made a mistake has never tried anything new."

(March 2024)

ROSE PRUNING – NO PAIN, NO GAIN

> "It is the time you have wasted for your rose that makes your rose so important."
>
> – Antoine de Saint-Exupéry (*The Little Prince*).

The rose, with its tender and beautiful flowers, but surrounded by sharp, harsh thorns appears in accounts from all of the world's major cultures and religions as a symbol of love at work in the world. In ancient mythology, roses symbolised eternal love in stories of how gods interacted with each other and human beings; in the Celtic/Druidic tradition, roses are used as decorations to represent the heart. Muslims view roses as symbols of the human soul: smelling the scent reminds them of their spirituality; whilst Hindus and Buddhists see roses as expressions of inner joy. Stories about roses often involve an inner spiritual journey – the prince in *Sleeping Beauty* has to cut through a forest of thorns to get to the palace; the songbird in Oscar Wilde's story, *The Nightingale and the Rose*, makes a sacrificial journey for a young man by singing love into a white rose, turning the rose red whilst impaled dying upon the thorns; Christ's final journey to the cross involves a crown of thorns.

So, a very special plant and quite rightly loved by us all; however, the variety of species and pruning techniques can be bewildering, and learning to understand and carry out these processes can be an inner journey in itself, sometimes complicated and sometimes painful, but one well worth taking. Traditionally, March is the best month to prune roses, once the worst of Winter damage of wind and frost has passed. Roses can be divided into three broad categories and each requires different pruning techniques – the main types are shrub roses, bush roses, and climbers/ramblers. Because the rose has had centuries of breeding, there are many variations within these three broad categories: there will be specific requirements for each sub-division, which can't be covered in this short article. There are, however, many websites that do go into this detail. Additionally, we are blessed with a wonderful rose nursery at nearby Wych Cross, with very knowledgeable staff that I am sure would be very happy to offer advice.

Shrub Roses

This category comprises most of the older varieties that existed before large-flowered bush roses or hybrid teas (see below) were introduced in the late nineteenth century. Most have simple flowers, and almost all flower just once on older growth in Summer. They can vary in size but are generally medium to large and have characteristic upright and often arching growth. Examples of shrub roses are the rugosas, the gallicas, the albas, plus moss roses and hybrid musks. Most of these varieties need only light pruning in Summer after flowering. They can be treated a bit like a shrub, where the older growth is removed to allow light and air into the body of the plant which will then encourage new growth. If the plant has become too large then reduce the tallest growths by about a third or so and, of course, as with all pruning, remove dead and dying branches.

Bush Roses

Since the late nineteenth century, plant breeding efforts have created many small-growing, compact, repeat-flowering roses suitable for bedding displays and small gardens. The large-flowered bush roses (hybrid teas) are remarkable for their shapely, high-centred flowers, double or single in a wide range of colours and scents; smaller-flowered bush roses (floribundas) are perhaps even more dramatic with their large trusses of flowers. Included in this category are also miniature and patio roses. Bush roses should be pruned in the early Spring (mid-March is ideal) before too much growth has occurred, but after most of the damaging frosts. Pruning consists of removing any dead or dying branches, as well as any weak or spindly growth. Remove anything that crosses or grows into the centre of plant as the aim is to create an 'open goblet' form to allow in light and air. The remaining strong, healthy stems should be cut to approximately 20cm from the ground, preferably to an outward-facing bud. If your bush rose is tall and in an exposed position then it is a good idea to reduce the whole plant by about a third in the Autumn to prevent wind-damage.

Climbers and ramblers

Once a climber or rambler has been established (usually against a wall or fence with the aid of wires), there is a reasonably simple procedure for annual pruning. Like bush roses, most climbers and ramblers flower on this year's growth, so pruning should be carried out in the dormant season before flowering. It is generally advisable to prune in Autumn for two reasons: 1) the young growth is more pliable; and 2) there is less damage caused by young shoots being blown around in the Winter wind (however, like all garden tasks, this is not set in stone – it is also fine to prune climbers throughout the Winter and on into March). Identifying young new growths is key to pruning success here – these strong green slender stems, often appearing from the base of the plant (a sign that the plant is vigorous and healthy) should be carefully trained into the existing framework. To make space for these growths, identify older less productive shoots as well as diseased and dying branches and remove carefully. A rule of thumb would be to remove about a quarter of older growth in any year. Look carefully and check twice before removing a seemingly 'old' stem, particularly on mature ramblers – sometimes such a stem supports a mass of young growth a good few metres away! Prune flowered shoots back by a few centimetres to a healthy bud and shorten any stems that have overgrown the rose's allotted space and tie in any new growth. Sometimes it may be necessary to reposition the arching stems to create a balanced framework on the wires.

No pain, no gain

Carrying out the varied techniques outlined above in order to achieve the prize of the best flowers will inevitably produce numerous cuts, scratches, and thorn-pricks (often surprisingly painful), even with the thickest of gloves. Perhaps by remembering the rose as the flower of love, pruning (complete with thorns), so necessary for healthy flowers, can be seen as a wider metaphor for bringing love into the world – not just in the garden but in our social life too: plants and people are both worth the effort! The old adage "no pain, no gain," suggested below by the authors Alphonse Carr, C. JoyBell C. and Anne Bronte respectively movingly and accurately describe this attitude:

> *"We can complain because rose bushes have thorns or rejoice because thorns have roses."*

> *"We all have thorns in our flesh. All of us. Love is when we stay and help someone pluck out their thorns one-by-one and they do the same for us. Love is also when we pluck the thorns out of our own flesh, one-by-one. But today, the world teaches us that we shouldn't even see those thorns, that we should only see the petals. As a result, we don't know how to love ourselves and we don't know how to love others. Stay with the darkness and bring that darkness into the light. It's there, look at it."*

> *"But he who dares not grasp the thorn, should never crave the rose."*

(March 2021)

MARCH

'ECO-HEAPS' REVISITED

"The ground's generosity takes in our compost and grows beauty, try to be more like the ground."

– Rumi.

In July 2020 I wrote about the processing of garden 'rubbish', introducing the idea of creating an 'eco-heap' in a corner of the garden where woody waste could be left to rot undisturbed – a process both labour-saving and ecological. In the last weeks, I have been working in a large eco-heap in one of my gardens and thought it would be interesting to revisit this idea.

I was prompted to address this corner for two reasons: firstly, it was overflowing with green waste of all kinds; and secondly, it looked very un-beautiful. What was going on?

The garden in question was the estate of Nutley Hall, a residential community for adults with special needs, and whilst I try, as one of the gardeners there, to keep the green waste processes in order, with a community of around 60 people it is sometimes an uphill struggle. The first thing I realised was that because it looked like a 'rubbish dump' it had been treated like one: all sorts of green waste – grass clippings, weeds, large logs and wooden crates had been deposited – none of which were supposed to be there. A 'vicious circle' had developed: where the more waste that was deposited, the more the heap looked untidy – which consequently attracted more waste!

Realising that I needed to take matters in hand by re-organising the heap, I made three further discoveries: the first was that in amongst the heap there was a reasonable quantity of perfectly good firewood (put there by myself!), the second was that a lot of the smaller wood had rotted to a beautiful mulch, and the third was that it had taken around five years to reach this state. Resolving to salvage the firewood and the mulch, I spent a good many hours sorting through the heap, until most had been removed and I could start rebuilding a new one on the existing site.

This time I have made it beautiful (in my eyes at least) from the outset, adopting the 'dead hedge' system widely used in the estate of Emerson College in Forest Row. This system utilises small pieces of woody material (up to 1cm in diameter), placed in an ordered way so that a low 'hedge' 50–75cm high is built. Once they reach the required height, no more material is added, indicating that the area is 'closed'. The positioning of the hedge is either along a live hedge line or a place where a visual barrier is required; these garden features are to my mind both beautiful and effective and are well worth a visit to Emerson College to see them.

So, to recap what I've learnt about an eco-heap:

- Position it somewhere where it can be left undisturbed for a long time (at least four to five years).
- Once built, don't keep adding new waste.
- Only put small woody material in the heap (up to 1cm in diameter).
- Make it as beautiful as possible – it is not a 'rubbish dump' (it could be a hedge, a pyramid, a dome…).
- Plan to use the compost once full rotting has taken place (some sieving may be required).

A final thought – one of the reasons that eco-heaps are 'ecological' is that they provide a home to insects and small mammals (particularly hedgehogs and mice). It is worth bearing this in mind when one reaches the point of using the compost: tread carefully and if one becomes aware that a little home is being disturbed, wait some time to allow any young to mature. The disturbance will probably prompt the animals to move to another location, so maybe have the new eco-heap near the old one to encourage a seamless move!

(March 2023)

APRIL

Into Action

Composting, weeding, lawn mowing, pruning and vegetable growing: everything happens now and everything is possible!

THE COMPOST HEAP – THE 'HEART CHAKRA' OF THE GARDEN

Although I have written about compost before (see *August 2020*), there are many ways of thinking about it; here is a slightly different approach celebrating another aspect of the heart chakra, which Glennie Kindred speaks of in relation to the mood and quality of the festival of Beltane which occurs at the very end of April.

APRIL

"This is the beginning of the [...] most actively potent part of the Earth's cycle. All of life is bursting with fertility and the power of its potential. This is the peak of the Spring season and the beginning of the Summer, when the Earth is clothed in green, the vibration of the heart chakra and love. Everywhere life is manifesting itself and moving outwards. [...] Beltane energy is one of reverence for all life. Reach out for what it is you want, everything is possible."

The ancient system of bodily chakras (or energy centres), which many of us know, lists seven main chakras: moving from the base of the spine – the root chakra, to the top of the head – the crown chakra, through the sacral, solar plexus, heart, throat and third eye. The heart chakra is in the middle and is the intermediary between the three lower and three higher chakras. Physically, it controls circulation, warmth and life itself. On an emotional level, it can regulate our likes and dislikes; and spiritually it can enliven our thinking.

But what has this to do with gardening? Well, quite a lot. We can think about a compost heap as a place of transformation: we are attempting to change 'waste' into 'nourishment'. We start with the 'lower' elements from the garden: food waste, weeds, grass clippings, shredded hedge materials and leaves – this 'rubbish' is often seen as an inconvenience, as something to get rid of. In my view, this is a mistake: our attitude to this 'waste' should be one of gratitude, as something with potential for creation. Now and then I can experience this, perhaps removing the weeds from garden beds in early May: chickweed, groundsel, cleavers; green, warm, moist and fragrant – almost good enough to eat! I take great pleasure in adding these to the compost, knowing how much life and goodness is within them. Turning to the chakra teachings of many spiritual teachers, we learn that the lower chakras (the root, sacral and solar plexus) often harbour trauma or energy which we feel uncomfortable with, which we perhaps don't want to acknowledge. They teach us that this, like the attitude to weeds outlined above, is also a mistake – we need to welcome this negative energy, and by welcoming it we can transform it. There are many techniques available to help with this transformation, clearly outside the scope of this article, but I would suggest they are all working with the same processes as composting!

Taking the chakra analogy just a little further, we can learn that enlivening our heart chakra through the process described above also then nourishes our higher chakras, our feelings of love, our way of speaking, of relating to each other and to the spiritual world. In other words, the lower feeds the higher. And in the garden? Well, the enlivened 'lower' waste properly cared for in the heap becomes food for the 'higher' flowers, fruit and seeds – which ultimately feeds both us and all the beings of the garden with the two streams of nourishment: that which we take in through our eyes, and that which we take in through eating.

Practical tips for composting:

A) Ensure there is a balance of woody and green material, dry and wet, and mix as often as you can.

B) Just like our hearts, the compost heap cannot accept everything – some things are difficult to compost effectively – couch grass, bindweed and ground elder should not be added but either burned or given to a local recycler able to compost at high temperatures. Cooked food waste and meat should also be avoided as this will encourage rats.

C) Allow time for transformation, at least six months is required for a heap to become useful.

D) Add biodynamic compost preparations. These six preparations made from common plants like dandelion, yarrow and nettle add an extra value to the heap, transforming the compost further, into something more than just food (see *www.biodynamic.org*).

E) The golden rule, again using the heart analogy, is to *love* your compost heap. A strange thought perhaps? But I believe that in doing this you will no longer look at it just as a place for putting 'rubbish', but rather as a place you love going to, and by loving it you will grow into instinctively knowing what your heap (your heart) desires!

(April 2022)

HOW GREEN IS YOUR GRASS? LAWN MOWING AND CLIMATE CHANGE

Many of us have grown up with the ideal lawn as a bright green, weed-free and low-growing area of grass; in some instances this is aesthetically, or practically appropriate – perhaps in a country house where the lawn shows off the architecture or in sport where turf quality is important, but from the point of view of climate change it is not ideal. Firstly, to obtain a lush, bright green lawn with no 'weeds', artificial fertilisers and weedkillers are required: these are produced in ways that create carbon dioxide – one of the gases that drives climate change. Secondly, weedkillers do what they say: kill weeds, but these 'weeds' are precisely the wildflowers that our dwindling bee and insect populations need for food. Thirdly, to achieve short grass, mowing needs to occur weekly and, whilst the majority of lawnmowers are still petrol-powered, the carbon footprint of this is high!

What is the solution? This is not easy, and it will be for each of us to find our own compromise. In my garden, I have divided the lawns into areas with different mowing regimes. The first is the 'lawn' – this is mown every two weeks, with no fertilisers or weedkillers. At different times of the year, beautiful low-growing wildflowers such as the blue bugle and the yellow birdsfoot trefoil appear, and they can be left for a week or two more before they are mown again – they are loved by insects and look very pretty! Weedkillers and fertilisers have never been used, and whilst there are patches of moss in between the grass and wildflowers, there is no problem with this natural coexistence. The second area is the 'wild meadow' – an intentional area of wildflowers that grows undisturbed from March until mid-August. Here I have sown a mix of native perennials: ox-eye daisies, vetch, wild carrot, etc. plus meadow grasses; this not only looks beautiful and attracts insects, but also needs no maintenance for six months. In mid-August the meadow is cut, with a lawnmower (on high cut), a strimmer or a scythe; from then until the end of the season it is mown fortnightly. The third area is the 'very wild meadow' – this is an area of lawn in a corner of the garden that has almost no annual maintenance. It is left to grow as a meadow throughout the Summer and then is allowed to 'grow old gracefully' into the Autumn and Winter with no mowing at all. I have introduced some native plants like ragged robin and devil's-bit scabious (an amazing blue Autumn-flowering perennial that continues until November!) and it is a real joy to watch the gentle Autumn mood of ageing flowers, drying seed heads and yellowing stalks complete with attendant insects. Admittedly, this area is the most 'untidy', so care in positioning it in your garden will be needed, but I am convinced that it is the most biodiverse, has the lowest carbon footprint for maintenance, and offers a possibility to observe the changing seasons close up.

When considering your own lawns, I would suggest the modest experimental approach: try a few small areas first to see how they grow and how you feel about them. If you like what develops then you can increase the size next year; if you don't, then try something else. Gardening, like Nature, is not meant to be a static process, it evolves!

A final thought: when the time comes to upgrade your lawnmower, it is worth considering battery-powered machines. Although every newly-made machine has a carbon footprint, and batteries also have an ethical cost, they are still greener than petrol mowers. For smaller areas, I would also recommend a scythe. This wonderful tool has a fourfold advantage: firstly, it uses no carbon-based fuel; secondly, it is super-quiet (no more disturbing your neighbours on a Sunday morning!); thirdly, it offers a wonderful physical and meditative workout; and fourthly, it keeps alive an ancient horticultural tradition.

Happy mowing!

(April 2020)

WEEDING RECONSIDERED

"To the merry man, every weed is a flower; to the afflicted man, every flower is a weed."

– Finnish proverb.

40 years ago, when I first trained as gardener in the Parks Department of Southampton City Council, weeding was a really important part of my day's work. Shrub beds were regularly treated with powerful (but now banned) weedkillers to control herbaceous weeds and grasses; other flower beds were regularly hoed and hand-weeded. The mark of a good flower bed was the beautifully turned brown soil, dead-level and with a fine crumb, which became a foil for the individual perennials or annuals within the bed. Looking back now, I realise that whilst there is some aesthetic value to this (the plants can be shown off to their 'best'), there are some very real concerns, both ecologically *and* aesthetically to this way of weeding.

Firstly – ecologically. There is now overwhelming scientific evidence to prove that the most living part of the soil, the top few centimetres, is healthy mainly because of the millions of mycorrhizal fungi that inhabit this layer. These fungal networks help plants take up valuable nutrients, protect them against pests and diseases, and help share out food between plants. Additionally, experiments have shown that the mycorrhizae act as a communication system – literally sending underground messages between plants, often at great distances; for example, warning each other of predators (just search this fascinating topic on the internet). So, every time we hoe or weed the soil we are damaging this really important natural resource and impoverishing our gardens. Another very obvious ecological step we can take is to never use weedkillers as they are always too poisonous to Nature – that's their job! Not only do they affect the soil, there is a wider ecological cost in the production of them in the first place, often involving heavily-polluting industrial processes and being marketed by the same companies who create bee-endangering pesticides.

Secondly – aesthetically. The idea of the garden as a showcase for individual specimen plants is a legacy from the Victorian era, where plant collecting was very popular. The gardens of Kew and Wakehurst are testimony to this – individual plants placed carefully within neatly weeded beds. Whilst there is a place for such gardens (to be able to observe a single specimen plant does have both scientific and aesthetic value), I would argue that much is lost. If we are attempting to bring Nature closer to us in our gardens, then one of the most important elements of Nature is its interconnectedness, or its intrinsic 'mixed-upness'. If we walk in Nature, nothing is separate – trees are never evenly spaced out, often even gloriously intertwined with each other, and shrubs, perennials and meadows are always in a relationship with many other plants. Additionally, and perhaps crucially, *there is never any bare soil*. Nature just doesn't do bare soil; for example, if a tree falls over leaving a bare patch where the root was, it will rapidly be colonised by a succession of plants. Therefore, if one of our aesthetic goals as gardeners is to recreate the feeling of Nature, then we may have to think twice about weeding and allow our gardens to become a little bit more 'natural'.

How can we practically do this in our gardens? Over the years, I haven't completely managed to stop weeding, but the amount of time spent on this occupation has significantly reduced from my time in the Parks Department. I think the first tip is to mulch any spare piece of open bare soil (for instance, in a newly planted border where space is initially required for the plants to fill out) – cover with grass cuttings, compost or well-rotted bark chips. Not only will this inhibit airborne weeds, it will also feed the soil and protect the plants against drought. Secondly, plant as close as you can – especially in the vegetable garden; research shows that closely planted vegetables do well, as long as the soil has good compost and mulch. Thirdly, when a weed does appear, think carefully about whether it needs to be removed – couch grass and other perennial weeds probably should, but what about leaving the daisy, the herb robert, and many other benign and interesting annual weeds? If we really want to be radical, and if time is limited, we could decide that all plants appearing in our gardens under 5cm can be called 'ground cover'! I have a few beds in my gardens with an amazing 'ground cover' plant, whose name I still don't know but whose flowers faithfully every year send up their pretty blue spikes from a network of dense cover, obviating a large amount of bare earth weeding. This is perhaps the ultimate in letting Nature take her course, or perhaps the art of 'conscious compromise', which I mentioned in an earlier article trying to find a balance between the needs of Nature and our needs as gardeners. This may involve more thought on our part and would need to be experimented with in our own gardens, but the rewards are great – more diversity, more mycorrhizae and hence more health; plus, the unexpected bonus – less work! This seems like something worth striving for.

(April 2021)

A SIMPLE VEGETABLE PLOT

Whilst most of my gardening work is ornamental (flowers, trees and meadows), I am occasionally asked to set up a simple vegetable plot within a garden; this year I am developing a small area about 3 x 8 metres on a piece of ground that used to be lawn. In the past, I would have stripped off the turf layer and then spent many hours moving the turf to a topsoil pile, digging the whole bed over and then raking it to a fine tilth. This was how I was taught to make beds for over 40 years whilst in the Parks Department and, although they look impressive (neat edges and freshly dug, level soil), they have many drawbacks. The first and most obvious is the amount of labour required – not just in the preparation, but also in the upkeep: once the soil is 'open', it needs attention in the form of constant weeding before the vegetables have become mature enough to do this job for me. The second problem is that by removing the turf and digging the soil, I am disturbing and depleting the rich mycorrhizal network that lives in the top few centimetres of soil, a network becoming more and more recognised as beneficial for soil health. Additionally, the useful air passages created by worms are removed, meaning that more artificial means will be needed to keep the soil aerated (hoeing, digging).

I was all set to continue with this system, but luckily was reminded by friends that there is another way – the no-dig vegetable garden championed by Charles Dowding. This is a simple and (hopefully) effective way of creating a vegetable plot from scratch with the minimum of effort and soil disturbance. I say, hopefully, because this is an experiment for me and even though I am assured it will work beautifully, I still feel a little uneasy changing my long-set habits! Below is the step-by-step process – in my case, on an existing lawn.

1. Mow the whole area on a low cut to remove as much growth as possible.

2. Mark out the bed dimensions.

3. Cover the whole area with a layer of cardboard, ensuring that there is a good 30cm strip around the edge, wider than the bed (this prevents encroaching grass and weeds). The cardboard should have as little ink and plastic as possible to minimise soil pollution. Large pieces are more effective and should overlap with their neighbours.

4. Cover with a thick layer of compost and leaf mulch, ideally up to 10cm. If paths are required, then wood/bark chips to a depth of 5cm be can added between beds, also with cardboard underneath.

5. A simple edge to hold the soil in is also recommended, thick straight branches of hazel or chestnut are ideal, but otherwise any scrap wood will work.

6. Any areas not immediately required can be covered with a semi-permeable weed membrane (weighted

with wood or bricks against the wind). This saves on unnecessary weeding of 'open soil', whilst being ready for new beds when the time comes.

I am reliably informed that this is all I need to do, and I can now plant directly into the soil. The question of whether or how the new plants can grow through the cardboard layer is interesting, I imagine that shallow-rooted plants like garlic will not have a problem and perhaps deeper-rooted herbaceous plants (e.g. herbs) might need a little help – with a small hole punched in the cardboard, whilst the cardboard is still strong. However, after a few weeks, particularly if it has rained, the cardboard will have become soft and it won't be a problem.

It's an interesting experiment for me – I'll report back throughout the next months how it works out in practice.

(April 2023)

THE HAZEL – BEAUTIFUL, GENEROUS AND USEFUL

Recently I needed to coppice a very mature hazel tree in one of the gardens where I work. The tree, though majestic and beautiful with striking catkins and patterned bark, was becoming too large and was overshadowing a nearby dwelling. After sawing each of the limbs down to the ground, and obviously being a little sad at having to cut back a living being so drastically, I reflected on the positive sides to the situation. Firstly, the removal of the five metre tree was hardly noticeable – being as it is in a grove of other hazels, which was a pleasant surprise, and it felt as though the remaining trees now had a little more light and air, as did the building nearby. Secondly, and most importantly, I reflected on the many uses of the cut stems – from the very largest to the smallest and realised how generous this plant is in the giving of their gifts. By cutting the tall stems right down to the ground (coppicing), I was continuing a tradition of plant husbandry that goes back many centuries. Coppicing has been practised by land-workers throughout the ages with native trees such as chestnut, hazel, willow, ash, alder and hornbeam. Alongside producing firewood from the largest stems, the hazel is a source of many other wooden items such as fence posts, tool handles, baskets, hurdles and walking sticks, as well as lobster pots and even the small Welsh fishing boat – the coracle. Once the tree has been coppiced, it is allowed to grow again unhindered for three or four years or more, when the process can be repeated. The trick I am learning in the management of this particular grove of hazels is to keep a constant succession of young and old wood – no easy task as I tend to err on the side of 'non-management', being reluctant to cut many trees, mistaking this for 'natural' and 'eco', when actually it is nothing other than a combination of laziness, forgetfulness, and misguided sentimentality! Remembering hazel's gifts helps me to realise that recycling and regeneration are also natural and are part of the co-creative process of being a gardener.

The products of this particular hazel weren't as wonderful as the items listed above, but nevertheless I used the whole plant, which was satisfying. The largest pieces of wood (around 12cm in diameter) have been saved for firewood, which will be dried thoroughly for a year before being burnt in an efficient wood stove. The next sizes (10–5cm diameter and very straight) have been put aside for tree stakes or large props for overhanging roses. Moving on to the 2cm diameter rods (2 metres in length and very supple): these have been collected and will be used throughout the year for simple fences around the garden – delineating areas without making a solid boundary – on road/path edges and near a small pond. I find the lightness of the bent sticks visually appealing as well as being practical. The final twiggy branches will be used for pea and bean sticks in the vegetable garden by simply pushing the ends into the soil – allowing the bushy flowering ends to support sweet peas, climbing peas and beans.

As a final flourish to the job, I collected a handful of the branches to put into a seasonal vase, knowing that the lovely lime green leaves will soon sprout alongside the pollen-filled golden catkins – reminding me of the generosity of this amazing tree. Autumn, of course, brings further joys – edible hazelnuts (also beloved by many birds and small mammals) and colourful leaves moving from browns and pinks to an ethereal yellow often lasting well into December; if you have space in a wooded corner of your garden, I would always recommend planting one or more of these wonderful trees, which offer their varied gifts throughout the year.

(April 2024)

MAY

Widening into Worldwide Life

Meditative gardening, a wonderful weed and plants as sovereign beings.

THE GARDEN IN MAY

"May, more than any other month of the year, wants us to feel most alive."

– Fennel Hudson.

In Spring 2020, when we suddenly experienced the curtailing of our outer freedoms through lockdown measures, I experienced a change in my attitude to Nature. Although there was no possibility of travelling or socialising, I was very fortunate to be able to continue gardening, working largely alone and outdoors. The skies and the roads were empty, and the sun shone for weeks through April and May, and as I worked, I remembered two experiences from earlier days. The first was from Switzerland where I worked with a team of vegetable and estate gardeners. The foreman, Benno, busy planning holidays, made the dramatic statement that no-one could go on holiday until Midsummer's Day (June 21st), an idea I didn't really understand or want to agree to. The second was a memory from my childhood of the smell of grass, lush Spring grass.

As I worked, for the first time in many years I slipped into a different way of being – apart from a day or two off during Easter, I took no holidays from March until mid-June. The experience was enlivening. Not only could I keep on top of the garden, but I felt more connected to the seasons and to all the plant growth – flowers, fruit, grass and 'weeds'. May in particular was truly 'a month to feel alive in', and as a gardener I then understood what Benno was suggesting and also my 'grass memory' – to be allowed to spend time undistracted by holidays, with Nature in all her lush aliveness was a gift. As Rudolf Steiner suggests in his *Soul Calendar*, we can feel into the light that shines in May and perhaps notice that:

> *"Within the light that out of spirit depths*
> *Germinating power is woven into space,*
> *Revealing the gods' creative work:*
> *Within its shine, the soul's true being*
> *Is widened into worldwide life,*
> *And resurrected*
> *From selfhood's narrow inner power."*
>
> *(Soul Calendar – 2nd week of May)*

This lovely idea of 'widening into worldwide life' will be my motif this May, and I will try to remember this, as the next weeks unfold towards Midsummer.

(May 2023)

CELANDINE – MY FAVOURITE 'WEED'

Early on in my gardening career I was responsible for an estate which had a large, neglected flower bed, which during April and May seemed to be predominantly full of the weed celandine (I knew it was a weed because I had learnt that at college, and I even knew which weedkiller was the most effective on it!). I needed to remove it because, after all, don't weeds need to be removed? It was an impossible task, particularly as I didn't use weedkillers: I spent two months digging, digging, digging. Below the soil were literally thousands of tiny little root nodules, looking a bit like eggs, and each one of these nodules could produce a new plant. After endless digging, I even resorted to a flame gun, carefully turning the soil to reveal the 'eggs' and then blasting them with fire! It was not successful… Most of the celandine remained until the end of May when it disappeared, only to come back the following year. Again, I would attack it as it was 'getting in the way' of my tidy 'Parks Department' style beds full of snapdragons and zinnias.

Looking back, I realise what a colossal waste of time and resources I used up trying to remove this beautiful 'weed'. Thirty years later, I work in a similar estate with similar flower beds, and guess what? They too are full of celandine!

But now I really appreciate this plant: not only does it bring its vibrant yellow in April, acting as a foil for other Spring plants like blue anemones but it also covers the soil, inhibiting water run-off and evaporation and preventing other weeds taking hold. In May, almost magically, it humbly disappears, leaving any bare soil ready to be over sown with Summer annuals. Additionally, by trying to remove the plant by digging, the vital mycelium network in the soil is unnecessarily damaged and, of course, it wastes a lot of time!

Perhaps this is a good lesson to learn – we now know that 'weeds' are only 'weeds' when they are in the wrong place, and I wonder if celandine can ever be in the wrong place with its humble and discreet manner and its manifold benefits? Admittedly, in an early Summer seed bed celandine might need to be removed, but where else? The reductive college education I received in the 1980's which wanted to separate everything into 'good' and 'bad' plants did not help: we weren't taught to look at the individual situation and observe the relationships between the plants. What is each plant doing in the bed? And what is the effect it has on the other plants? For me, gardening is about these relationships, not necessarily seen at the beginning, but discovered when I am patient and observant, and when I don't bring a fixed idea to the situation. I remember now when I was busy all those years ago trying to remove the celandine, someone suggested to me that the plant was trying to teach me something. At the time, I roundly dismissed this idea, preferring to believe in my own 'truth'; but now, I realise they were probably right.

News from the Vegetable Garden

Last month I wrote about the 'no-dig' vegetable garden I have been developing, and I wanted to give a short update. So far, so good: everything seems to be progressing as it should – the garlic and beans are growing well, and I can only assume that they have found their way through the cardboard and into the soil below. In April I planted potatoes and onions just an inch above the cardboard, at the time of writing I cannot tell how they are doing. There are very few weeds anywhere yet, so the cardboard seems to be successful; however, I imagine that May with all her lush growth will bring some weed challenges, particularly on the edges of the beds and as the cardboard slowly disappears. I will ask my friendly advisors what the next step would be to reduce weeds – my feeling is to plant really densely to minimise open soil. For example, sowing carrots between the onions, and annual flowers like calendula between squashes and tomatoes. Additionally, I will probably need to keep the grass and other plants around the edge cut as low as possible. To be continued …

(May 2022)

WHY WE NEED TO RECOGNISE PLANTS AS SOVEREIGN BEINGS (PLANT HEALTH PART 1)

A few weeks ago I was asked by someone starting out in horticulture if I could tell them the main diseases that I have come across whilst gardening. This came as a surprise to me, and I had to think hard before answering. This was partly because I don't think about disease much and also because I haven't had much experience of garden diseases. I think the two facts might be related … (more later). I racked my memory; all I could come up with was that a customer I knew had lost a cherry tree to silver leaf (a fungal disease that can affect stone fruit if they are pruned in the Winter), and a local chestnut that was affected by bleeding canker. Otherwise, I didn't have much to report – unless you consider 'black spot' on rose leaves a disease? Apparently it is, but I prefer to call them just black spots. They don't seem to harm the rose very much, the flowers continue to be beautiful and they don't seem to die over the Winter, so maybe we don't need to worry? Perhaps we are looking in the wrong direction? The same with those amazing orange blotches on pear leaves in August – very beautiful, but are they disease? Maybe … but the pears seem happy.

I am aware that this attitude to plant disease could be considered reckless and perhaps a little lazy (there is some truth in the latter, I prefer to sit in a garden rather than work!) and seems to fly in the face of conventional wisdom about health, but it has served me well over 40 years of gardening. When people ask me how to help a 'diseased' plant, my answer is always the same: prune any dead bits off, ensure they have a good amount of light and air all around them, feed the soil with homemade organic compost, make sure they have enough water and ask them what they might need. This seems to work, and I don't think that I have left a trail of dead and diseased plants behind me!

The practice of conversing with plants, alive in all indigenous cultures around the world (including our own Celtic tradition), is now becoming accepted and worked with again here in Western societies, and I now believe that my inner attitude to plants is just as important as my outer actions. Plants do respond to our conversations with them and are grateful for this recognition and respect – they are sovereign beings. Instead of treating a plant as something that gets ill and then needs to be cured by human-made medicine (pesticides, fungicides, etc.), we can enter into respectful dialogue with them and together create the best conditions for health. If we can't yet hear what they say, then maybe we could just hazard a guess … Generally, it is (no surprises!): light, air, food, water and respect.

My time at agricultural college in the 1980's was not a particularly inspiring time with regard to plant health and disease: we had to learn countless diseases alongside their chemical remedies, together with the obligatory long list of cancer-inducing weedkillers. We looked at the plant as an object that needs to be cared for and cured as if it was ill, coming out of a mind-set that could be called controlling and patriarchal. We knew what the plants needed if they became ill, and we could save them; but did we ever ask if they needed saving with our pharmaceutical ideal? Perhaps as sovereign beings they didn't need this? An example of this alternative attitude at our horticultural college was Mr. Broad, a newly appointed tree surgeon whose approach to plant health seemed revolutionary at the time. A shambling sort of 'hippy' who smoked roll-ups and enjoyed leisurely lunches, he explained that if we had to prune a branch off a tree then we didn't need to apply fungicide and a paint that 'sealed' the wound, that protected it from 'germs', mirroring the idea of the sticking plaster (and which was a very prevalent view in those days). No, we didn't need to do anything. The tree was perfectly able to heal themselves, there are numerous processes within the tree that enable healing, particularly the callusing that occurs after a branch has fallen or has been cut (admittedly, it is important to make the pruning cut appropriately at an angle to enable rain to run off and also to leave the branch collar intact to allow the trees own healing substances to work, but still, minimal aftercare). He showed us that plants as sovereign beings know what to do – they have been around a lot longer than us! (walking in our own Ashdown Forest) we can notice the many branches that have fallen off trees, with wounds that look jagged and raw – but which all heal beautifully, untouched by human hand.

We could try this in our gardens … Apart from reducing the amount of chemical plant "medicine" on the shelves of our garden centres, medicine that is created by the same chemical and petroleum companies driving climate change, we will save money, save energy by shopping less, bring respect into our plant relationships and maybe feel happier and more content as a result. Perhaps we can think about plant illness less, and think about sovereign plant health more, and by doing this we develop a new kinder energy for health to naturally arise in Nature.

NB: as well as the five fundamental qualities mentioned above, there is certainly a place in our gardens for plant-based remedies of teas and preparations for plant health. Contrary to pharmaceutical plant medicines of the last century, which work with a 'top-down' view of plant health, these remedies have arisen from millennia of respectful co-working with Nature as described above, and which will be discussed in Part 2 next month.

(May 2021)

JUNE

The Sun's High Hour

More meditative gardening, the lovely rose and resilient, healthy plants.

THE GARDEN IN JUNE

"*In this the sun's high hour it rests
With you to understand these words of wisdom:
Surrendered to the beauty of the world,
Be stirred with new-enlivened feeling;
The human I can lose itself
And find itself within the cosmic I.*"

(Soul Calendar – 3rd week of June)

In June, the cycle of the year has reached it's 'high hour', the sun being at her highest point in the sky with long and hopefully warm, sunny days full of the scent of roses and other blossoms. To a certain extent, my work as a gardener shifts into a different gear: the non-stop growth of May now subsides a little – lawns and meadows become different as the grasses and other plants change from vigorous growth of green stems to flowering and the beginning of seed creation, fruit trees and bushes have blossomed and are now beginning to create their first fruit buds, the flowers in the beds come to the fore and are now in their full glory – roses, peonies, lilies, irises, phloxes, hydrangeas, and many others. Somehow the weeds of May have subsided a little too, and for my garden work there also seems to be a possibility of a gentle pause.

This pause could take the form of a short holiday, or even just taking time out: sitting, eating, entertaining in the garden. We can, of course, do this throughout the year, there are no rules about when we can relax, but for me 'surrendering to the beauty of the world' at Midsummer is a special feeling; and perhaps by doing this in a meditative way, I might sense the Spirit in Nature (the 'Cosmic I') that informs and pervades all that we see around us in our gardens and landscapes. Interestingly, the sun herself makes a pause on Midsummer's Day (June 21st); this day is also known as the Summer Solstice, where the sun ('sol') stands still ('stice'). If she is doing this then I think we are in good company, and to celebrate this moment either alone or with friends feels like a good idea!

June Garden Work

The pauses and celebrations around Midsummer will always be tempered a little by the June gardening tasks, some of which are listed below; however, none of them seem too arduous compared to the busy times of Spring and again in the Autumn.

- Prune wisteria shoots at the end of June after flowering, to 6–8 inches, to encourage next year's flowers and prevent excessive growth.
- Prune other early flowering shrubs – ribes, forsythia, philadelphus and weigela as soon as they have flowered. These shrubs flower on the previous season's growth, so now is the time to encourage growth and flower buds for next year.
- Trim hedges very lightly, allowing them to stay a bit flowing and alive in appearance (check for late nesting birds first).
- Support tall-growing perennials with sturdy canes – use local hazel ideally, or otherwise bamboo.
- Cut back Spring-flowering perennials like pulmonarias and geraniums, to encourage a further flush of flowers.
- Water newly established plants regularly, but also keep a check on all your plants: even mature plants can suffer from drought – in my experience cherries, roses and rosemary have all suffered in previous hot Summers. Additionally, keep ponds, wetlands and birdbaths topped-up, these habitats are crucial to many different creatures in our gardens – dragonflies who will now be emerging from the water, the hedgehog on her nightly round, and the various birds who love to bathe and drink from these water features. Additionally, many mammals including badgers and foxes (and even domestic cats) will use a pond as a place to drink from.

And the No-dig Veg Plot...?

Fingers crossed it's all going well, everything seems to be growing in the right direction ... roots downwards through the compost and cardboard, shoots upwards into the light! Perhaps because of the wet Spring, no watering has yet been required; but it might also be due to the thick compost and the mulching aspect of the cardboard below? I imagine that this might change as we move into high Summer and the beginnings of the fruiting and ripening process ...

(June 2023)

JUNE – THE MONTH OF THE ROSE

"It was June, and the world smelled of roses. The sunshine was like powdered gold over the grassy hillside."

– Maude Hart Lovelace.

This time last year I was busy preparing for a weekend-long 'rose initiation journey' with Pam Montgomery, an American-based plant spirit healer. The journey was profound and inspiring, and required the creation of a variety of tinctures from local roses dear to me, combined into an elixir that was drunk throughout the weekend. Using a combination of shamanic practices including meditation, observation, guided discussion and journeying, we were led both individually and collectively to meet the Spirit of Rose. Amongst many other teachings I received during this weekend was how selfless and loving Rose is and how she asks us to learn to love ourselves as much as we can. Perhaps, without even having to go on an 'initiation journey', we can sense this anyway – those of us who surround ourselves with her beauty by planting roses in our gardens may notice that roses touch our hearts like no other plant.

A year has now passed and the roses are now returning. In June, many will be in full flower; so, in the spirit of gratitude to this most selfless and generous being, I want to list three of my favourite roses.

The Apothecary Rose

Perhaps my all-time favourite, I planted this 3ft high shrub rose (Rosa gallica/officinalis) in my garden about ten years ago and she has gently spread throughout the flower bed with her simple suckering habit. The suckers (underground runners producing new growth) are a problem – not because they can't be removed easily, but because each new growth brings more irresistible flowers, which, for the sake of the other plants, I have to force myself to remove! She has deep pink flowers with yellow centres, highly scented, that vibrantly contrast with lime green leaves. The rose originated from Persia and came to Europe in the twelfth or thirteenth century, via returning knights in the Crusades. It was the most commonly cultivated rose in Europe until the 1800's and has many healing properties. She flowers only once, in June, but the display lasts a good few weeks and is enough for me for the whole year.

Climbing Rose "Lovers Meeting"

The name, perhaps, says it all – this well-behaved climber produces the most exquisite and perfect orange flowers borne on single firm stems; and is ideal for cutting, even a single bloom given as a gift feels like something special.

Her flowers will last many days in a vase and although not scented, the rose is a prolific repeat flowerer, last year offering two very long flowering seasons. She grows in my garden against a pale pink exterior wall and the combination of the deep orange blooms with the young copper leaves is stunning in May and June.

Rose "Tottering by Gently"

This last one is a little different as I do not know her very well yet (!) but is included because of a recommendation by a gardening colleague whose rose appreciation I greatly respect. At his suggestion, I recently planted five in a rejuvenated flower bed and they are presently just sprouting green shoots; my colleague says she is, amongst other qualities, 'ethereal', 'light', 'gentle', 'fresh' and 'Spring-like'. The company who bred the rose, David Austin Roses, says that "its beauty is found in the simplicity of its single yellow flowers and the spectacular display they create when viewed en-masse. They are held in large, open sprays on a rounded, branching shrub." They are disease resistant, bee-friendly, with a light musk scent. I am hoping that the repeating blooms rising out of ground-cover geraniums will add an eye-catching and enduring jewel-like quality to the front of the flower bed.

Time will tell …!

(June 2022)

HOW CAN WE HELP PLANTS HEAL THEMSELVES? (PLANT HEALTH PART 2)

In my last article I suggested that in my experience plants don't get ill very much and that if they do, the first things we can offer are some simple interventions: pruning dead wood, thinning for light and air, watering and feeding the plant and the soil. Sometimes, however, further help may be required; this article will introduce the most common plant-based remedies that may help plant health, as well as an introduction to biodynamic preparations.

Whilst having extensively used biodynamic preparations, I have not used many of the plant teas and liquid manures, preferring to trust in Nature's own healing processes. However, it seems to me that this might be a good subject to learn more about: helping plants heal themselves. This knowledge has existed throughout the centuries, preserved carefully by the countless land-healers in all cultures around the world, who use their own local, native plants to bring health, harmony and vitality to their surroundings.

Equisetum

Equisetum (horsetail) tea can be used against mildew, which starts as a grey-blue sheen on the underside of leaves. Mildew is damaging because it draws off nutrients from the plant, eventually causing the leaves and/or buds to drop off; potato and tomato blight, plus rose mildew are some of the most common types encountered in our gardens. Mildew spreads primarily under moist and warm conditions with too little air and is often found in greenhouses. Equisetum as a remedy can counter this warm moistness – the sharp crystalline forces of the horsetail, observable in their thin strong growth pattern, helps to bring balance to the moisture that caused the mildew. To make this tea, we will need to add the plant to cold water, bring to boil and leave to simmer for half an hour or so. To make the tea more effective, include some crushed pieces of oak bark. Use a 1:10 dilution (1 part tea, 10 parts water).

Comfrey

Comfrey is probably the star of herbal remedies. Not only is it beautiful, creating good ground cover and being attractive to bees, but it contains a multitude of nutrients including nitrogen, phosphorous, potassium, potash and calcium, as well as many trace elements like boron – vital for flowering and fruit setting. Comfrey liquid manure can be used as a general feed for the soil and the plants to maintain health. It acts like a tonic, helping plants stay healthy or strengthening those who have become weak due to illness or pest attack.

To make a liquid manure, add 1kg of comfrey leaves to 10 litres of rainwater and leave to ferment for 4–10 days (I have been reliably informed that it is best to put the comfrey leaves in a net or sack to allow ease of removal, and also that it has a very pungent smell!). The resultant liquid manure can be diluted 1:10 before applying it to the soil around our plants. Diluted further (1:20), it can be used as foliar feed to reduce stress, particularly after extreme weather – drought or hailstorms, for example. This can be applied with a sprayer or watering can with a fine rose.

Nettle

Nettle is also very rich in life-giving nutrients: iron, magnesium, calcium and potassium and can be used as a preventative remedy against pests (aphids on fruit trees) and diseases (chlorosis – leaves turning yellow in stressed situations), as well as a general preventative feed to encourage vitality. To make nettle tea, add the leaves to boiling water and allow to infuse for ten minutes. Spray the cold (diluted to 1:10) tea onto the leaves of the affected plant (NB: adding nettle leaves, again in their own sack, to the comfrey liquid manure described above will enhance even more the health-sustaining properties of this plant tonic.

Tansy

In the book, *Biodynamic Gardening* by Monty Waldin, tansy (Tanacetum vulgare) is stated to be "a useful addition to the garden, it not only attracts beneficial insects but also repels pests. A strategically placed clump of fresh tansy leaves, stems and flowers can help keep ticks and fleas away from the dog basket, and mites away from bedroom linen. [....] Tansy is prepared as a cold extract: soak a couple of heaped handfuls of chopped leaves in 1 litre of cold rainwater for two days, and then strain and spray without diluting." This extract is useful against rust and mildew, also prevents whitefly on brassicas and codling moth on ripening fruit. I have never used this remedy and in fact I don't know the plant that well, but it sounds like a really helpful remedy which I will look into.

Biodynamic Preparations

In the Forest Row area, Tablehurst and Plaw Hatch Farm, Emerson Garden, Brambletye Fruit Farm and Orchard Eggs are some of the hundreds of farms, smallholdings and gardens in Britain that follow biodynamic principles. Biodynamics is a fully holistic approach to gardening and farming, taking in everything from the smallest microbe in the soil to the furthest constellation in the night sky. Biodynamic land-workers see themselves as partners with the soil and their plants and animals, and by using carefully developed preparations, they work with and enhance the natural health regulation properties inherent in all living organisms.

'Horn Manure' and 'Horn Silica'

These are the two core preparations, made from cow manure and ground silica respectively. I spray them just three times a year: 'horn manure' in Spring and Autumn, and 'horn silica' in early Summer, which could be seen as a basic minimum. Other growers and farmers carry out more sprays throughout the year and use a variety of timings and combinations to achieve specific results, but this is outside the scope of this article.

'Horn manure', sprayed onto the soil in the afternoon, stimulates soil vitality and encourages plants to connect with the specific conditions of their growing site, a simple way of strengthening a plant's own natural resilience. It also encourages deeper rooting systems, increased earthworm activity and a better retention of soil moisture – all qualities advantageous to plant health.

'Horn silica', sprayed in the early morning, directly onto the leaves of growing plants, enhances the qualities of growth and maturation, bringing a warming element to the garden and helping to stabilise and balance plant metabolism – again all advantageous in helping a plant stay healthy (it can be applied later in the year too to food crops to aid plant ripening and increase nutritive value).

Compost Preparations

Made from six native plants (yarrow, nettle, chamomile, dandelion, oak bark and valerian), these are used to treat compost heaps; their purpose is to regulate the many organic processes taking place within an active heap. Each preparation has its own unique function in relation to the various soil nutrient processes and once the compost is spread on flower or vegetable beds, it brings balance, resilience and life to plants – again ultimately helping them help themselves.

In my experience, using the two sprays and the compost preparations over a number of years, brings a subtle and growing feeling of 'self-sufficient' health to a garden, as if the plants are able to find the 'key' to themselves and to their environment. It does not happen overnight, patience is required, but it is a very rewarding and inspiring co-creative experience to see plants growing healthily and in tune with Nature, both outwardly and inwardly. Additionally, I suspect that using the teas and liquid manures described above, alongside the biodynamic preparations, will have an even more beneficial effect – something I will definitely experiment with in the coming years.

For further information on biodynamic gardening, including purchasing and using the preparations, see the Biodynamic Association's website: *www.biodynamic.org*

(June 2021)

JULY

The Dance Changes

Working with Nature, ending the 'war on weeds', new thoughts on lawns and the tree as a sacred being.

EFFICIENT, ETHICAL AND COST-EFFECTIVE – TEN GARDEN TIPS FOR JULY

Now that the flush of June has taken place, where gardeners have had to dance in her vigour and beauty, we can now relax a little and reflect on how the year in our garden has been so far, perhaps noting new ways of future working. The expectancy for the first roses – now here amongst us, the worry about fruit set through the frosty times – now hopefully swelling gently on the branches, and the hard work of transferring the wonderful, succulent weeds from the garden beds to the compost heap, adding richness and vitality, can now all be laid to one side as we can take some time out to reflect. For me, it is becoming increasingly clear that I want to work *with* Nature, instead of *against* Nature, so I am always looking for simple ways to realise this ideal. Additionally, I am happy if I can do this efficiently without too much financial expense and as ethically as possible; below are some simple suggestions drawing on these ideals.

1) Use hazel poles instead of bamboos for plant supports. Hazels are very plentiful in our area and if we cut the poles that we require in Spring, the plants will have a chance to regrow for the following year. Either cut back the whole plant down to the ground (coppicing), or simply choose stems of the right thickness from a more mature plant. Thin poles (approx. 1cm diameter) are good for staking sunflowers and other annuals; thicker ones (3–4cm diameter) work for edible peas, plus runner beans, etc. The advantage of hazel is that young plants find the stems easier to grow up, being rougher than bamboo; additionally, because most bamboos are imported, they have an inherent carbon footprint (air miles) and are generally not fairly traded, meaning that workers who produce them may not receive a living wage.

2) Cut docks before they seed. An old country saying about docks runs: "One year of seeds give seven years of weeds." Dock seeds are very resilient and long-lived (archaeologists have discovered viable dock seeds in excavated Roman remains!), so it is a good idea to remove any dock flowers in June and July before they set seed. It is not always possible to remove the whole plant at this busy time, but it is relatively simple to just cut the tops off when passing and put them in the compost (if the seeds are ripe, then it would be safer to burn them or put in the green waste bin).

3) Feed birds all year round. The RSPB recommend feeding birds throughout the year (with the proviso not to put out large chunks of bread or loose peanuts which many be a choking hazard for fledglings), as this will encourage regular garden visits. This is not only a lovely thing – beauty and song for us, but also very ecological – birds love garden 'pests'. There is a climbing rose in our garden that is regularly visited by a pair of nesting blue tits who seem to be very happy eating the greenfly, meaning that we generally don't need to worry about more invasive, poisonous and expensive chemical pest control.

4) Use cardboard toilet rolls as pots. For next year's peas and beans, we can collect used cardboard toilet rolls and use them for pots. This is super-efficient, cheap and ethical as the rolls not only encourage the necessary deep rooting of the legumes, but they can also be planted directly into the soil, thus minimising root disturbance – and a few less plastic pots are created, circulated and then discarded. A small but simple step to help reduce the ever-growing plastic waste crisis.

5) Water compost. In dry weather, it will be necessary to water our compost heaps and bays, or they will dry out and the decomposing process will stall. Rainwater is best – just sprinkle with a watering can now and again and mix it all up with a fork, as if making a cake: not too wet and not too dry. For very dry periods, it might be necessary to use a hosepipe and drench for longer. Healthy, well-rotted home compost is a simple, efficient and cheap alternative to plastic-wrapped compost transported to us with its small but real carbon footprint. Add the biodynamic compost preparations (see last month's article on *Plant Health*) for even more vitality.

6) Mulch beds. If there is any bare soil in our flower or vegetable beds then it is always good to mulch with compost, grass, rotted leaves: anything to cover the soil – it is a simple and effective way of suppressing weeds and retaining moisture.

7) Collect animal manure. Animal manure (except from cats and dogs, which contains harmful pathogens) is wonderful for the compost heap. Cow manure is the very best, having been transformed by the animal's complex digestion process; but horse, rabbit, guinea pig and chicken manure is fine too (horse manure can even be collected off the street – super-efficient!). The manure is mixed in with the rest of the 'compost cake' ingredients and left to 'cook' for a few months. Organic or at least 'chemical free' manure is of course preferable but, in my view, any local animal manure is better than no manure.

8) Hoe regularly. Although an ideal garden will have little if any bare soil, there are some situations, particularly in the vegetable garden, where this is impractical. Regular hoeing (preferably with a bronze implement, see below) will keep weeds at bay; in the Summer the small cut seedlings can be left on the soil to dry out in the sun, so we won't need to remove them.

9) Become friends with slugs. Slugs are less attracted to soil that has been worked with a bronze tool (containing an amount of copper). By using such tools, the slug will often choose to go elsewhere: a simple and friendly way of dealing with them, obviating more radical measures like poison or drowning in beer. This is not a foolproof method, but my experience suggests that there is a reduction in slugs after using bronze tools (see my website for a range of the most common tools available).

10) Make herb tea. If we have planted mint, sage or lemon balm (all very easy to grow), either in small pots (mint) or in the herb garden, then at the end of the day we can sit back and enjoy our own freshly picked herb tea. We could also venture further into the local meadows for other herbs: my personal favourite is a meadowsweet and thistle mix. Pick a sprig of creamy meadowsweet together with a single young blue thistle flower (which dyes the tea a beautiful blue) and add to boiling water – a wonderful Summer tea. Local, in season and free throughout the months of July and August, and harvested on an evening walk across the local meadow – this tea ticks all the boxes!

(July 2021)

"WHAT SHALL WE DO WITH ALL THIS RUBBISH?" – HOW TO END THE 'WAR ON WEEDS'

As a gardener, I often hear this question; no matter how much we prune, cut and clear, Nature creates ever more growth, particularly at this time of year when her growth forces are strong. We can feel overwhelmed with all this 'rubbish', perhaps resorting to frequent bonfires, filling our recycling bins or trips to the dump in a desperate attempt to keep on top of it. We can feel that we are 'at war' with the garden, trying to hold back the tide of growth. But it needn't be like this, perhaps the solution is to ask a different question: not "what shall we do with all this rubbish?" but rather "is this really 'rubbish' and if not, perhaps it is something useful, a gift for us and our garden?" By asking this simple question, we are no longer at 'war with the weeds' as we begin to change our point of view. Below is a list of all the 'rubbish' that with only a few exceptions can remain in the garden and be very useful.

Woody Material: If you are pruning trees, shrubs and woody plants then there are many ways of using this material. Any branch larger than 3cm (just over 1 inch) diameter is perfect firewood. If seasoned and dried properly, they can be used in an energy-efficient wood-burning stove. If you don't have one yourself then ask friends or neighbours – most people would be delighted to receive your gift. For branches between 3cm and 1cm in diameter, the best thing for these is to create an 'eco-heap' in your garden. Choose a spot in a corner under some larger shrubs or trees and build a heap with your prunings; it doesn't have to be beautiful, but it can be (at Great Dixter in Kent they have built extremely attractive large eco-heaps, designed to be admired!). I would suggest limiting the heap to just one season's worth of wood and then moving to a new area the following season. These heaps are havens for wildlife; particularly insects, but also the increasingly rare hedgehog, as well as a range of fungi. The heap should then be left undisturbed; perhaps carefully treading it down once a year (in the Summer, when no hedgehogs will be hibernating) until it naturally disappears over a few years. Prunings below 1cm in diameter can be chopped by hand or with a lawnmower and added to the compost heap.

Weeds: Apart from the three 'difficult' weeds: dock, bindweed and ground elder, all other weeds can be put on your compost heap. As long as the heap is hot enough from a good mix of different materials then most weeds will compost well and they contain valuable trace elements. Dock, bindweed and ground elder should not be directly composted until they have been treated with a 'stewing' process. A deep bucket or barrel filled with water provides a good place for stewing: add the weeds to the water and allow at least six weeks for full rotting to take place – they will be a bit smelly, but they can now be added to the compost heap, again providing valuable nutrients (NB: if the dock has produced seeds, then these should *not* be added to the stew, rather dry and burn them on a bonfire).

Grass Clippings: As long as the grass is added to a compost heap which has a good mix of other (dryer) materials, it is excellent in providing warmth, moisture and nitrogen. If you have too much then you can use it as a mulch around vegetables and other plants: invaluable in dry weather to retain moisture and prevent weed growth.

Leaves: Small amounts can go directly into the compost, but if you have too many then a separate leaf compost area will be required. Most leaves take two years to fully rot down (compared to a six month compost heap), so putting leaves either in a simple wire frame or a box would be ideal. You would need at least two separate containers to allow for the two year rotting process. Leaves, like weeds and grass are extremely high in nutrients for the garden.

The two exceptions to the above are bamboo and Japanese knotgrass – both highly invasive perennials that can spread rapidly; they should not be composted, nor given to the Council for recycling. The two ways of removing them are either with a weedkiller or by digging and burning. I do not recommend weed-killing as the active ingredient in such weedkillers is glyphosate, which is highly likely to be harmful to bees, soil health and is cancer-inducing; the other way is by digging and burning. It is labour-intensive and will require a few years to completely eradicate, but it is possible. Once you have removed the roots, dry them out for a few weeks and then burn them on a bonfire (for more information on identification and safe disposal of Japanese knotgrass please see: www.gov.uk).

By questioning our views on 'rubbish' we not only reduce our carbon footprint (less trips to the dump and less bonfires) but we also increase the nutrient value of our garden, as well as providing more biodiversity. With the realisation that there are very few 'bad weeds' we can look at our garden in a different way: as no longer something that creates problem rubbish for us to deal with, but rather a place of mutual benefit where our garden helps us as we help the garden. We no longer feel separate from Nature and 'at war with the weeds' but begin to sense a certain deeper connectedness with her as we discover her gifts.

Happy weeding!
(July 2021)

NO-MOW MAY (... AND JUNE, JULY?)

I am aware of the admirable suggestion from ecologists of the concept of 'No-Mow May' as a way of increasing biodiversity and encouraging more wildlife into our gardens. The practice is a simple one – we stop mowing lawns for the month of May to encourage the hidden wildflowers within the grass to come to prominence. Depending on the soil, these could be daisies, clovers, buttercups, bird's-foot trefoil and speedwell. At the end of May, we mow this again (it's not yet too tall for lawnmowers) and return the lawn to its original cropped green. A simple, efficient and rather delightful way to bring bees and other insects right up close to us with no effort – saving time and also reducing our fuel costs.

As someone who has planted meadows in most of the gardens I work in, I thought that 'No-Mow May' didn't apply to me. I have written previously about creating small islands, patches, strips of wildflower meadow and contrasting these with 'normal' lawns that are mown regularly. I have to admit that this does look pleasing and feels good – we see the biodiversity of the meadow and also the neatness of the lawn and they seem to work well together. However, last month (mid-May), one of my clients said to me: "What about 'No-Mow May', shouldn't we do it here?" My initial reaction was that I was 'exempt' from this because of the number of wildflower patches and meadows already in existence there (it's a small estate), but later I thought: "Well, why not?" Some of the lawns are not used extensively for play or sitting, so it might be possible to allow flowers to come for at least a few weeks.

It is now mid-June and having returned from a week's break I find the lawns alive with insects, predominantly bumblebees, who are feeding on the huge, gorgeous patches of red and white clover that have sprung up as if by magic. Whilst there is a need for some access – shed, washing line, back door to kitchen, which is facilitated by some judicious and slightly tortuous path mowing – the rest is still standing. Admittedly, the contrast between the traditional taller meadow and short cut grass is less obvious, but at the moment at least, the benefits seem to outweigh the costs. So, I'm leaving it. How long for? … I'm not sure. Until the client asks me to mow it? Until it looks too long for a mower? Until it looks unattractive?

Marjoram, my Favourite Herb

The concept outlined above of leaving a plant standing in the garden until it looks unattractive has been used by me in extremis with marjoram. Having decided to keep the beautiful dead flower heads over the Winter, complementing grasses and other foliage, I was presented with the dilemma – when should I cut the heads? April turned into May, which turned into June, and still the stalks stood. There just never seemed to be a good time to cut them as they, to my eye, still looked attractive. At the time of writing (mid-June), the new flower stalks are inching their way up and will, soon, overgrow the old stalks – so it looks like they won't be cut this year! Good or bad? I'm not sure…. The crisp pruning can in some instances look attractive but, in my case, the dead flower heads won!

And why is marjoram my favourite herb? Well, the flowers are a beautiful pink, with a long season and they are one of the top bee-attractors in the garden (as long as you choose the native variety – Origanum vulgare). Additionally, as well as being very easy to propagate by seed, they spread well – quickly creating a dense but not-suffocating aromatic green mound. They are generous: one can easily take a small clump and transplant it with minimal damage to the mother-plant; and, of course, marjoram is a wonderful herb for the kitchen – useful for many Italian and Greek dishes, especially pizzas, but can also be used in soups and salads. A wonderful all-round herb for the mixed flower garden.

(July 2022)

TREES IN THE GARDEN

As we head into the warmest time of the year – July and August, I want to give a moment of gratitude towards trees, using the words of Glennie Kindred in her book, *The Sacred Tree*:

> *"Once trees covered this land and were revered and honoured as important powerful lifeforms. For thousands of years, humankind has relied on the abundance of trees for much of their material needs, from the air that we breathe, fire to keep us warm, many kinds of industry, wood for our buildings and transport, medicine and food.*
>
> *Throughout the world, trees have become recognised as living beings who have a spirit within. There is much documentation of country lore, customs, ceremonies and procedures for felling trees. Most of this is ignored today, but still foresters have many tales of understanding and awareness of the tree kingdoms' inherent presence. Anyone who walks in the woods appreciates the special atmosphere of the trees, knows in their hearts of their power and living energy."*

To the above list of good qualities of trees I could add two more: shade and wildlife habitat. As I write this on a beautiful but very warm June morning, I appreciate both the shade of the mighty oaks and birches who surround my garden and the song of birds who live within and around these trees. I feel very fortunate to be surrounded by these ancient wise beings, selflessly offering their shade and shelter to us and the animals that live near us.

Although many people are worried about the negative effects of trees planted in gardens – blocking out light, too many leaves to clear in Autumn, and damage to house foundations, by careful choice of species and appropriate positioning most of these problems can be avoided. Clearly it would be inadvisable to plant a willow with her foundation-undermining roots close to your home or drainage systems, as would planting a large oak or beech near a boundary if that boundary is close to a neighbour: in twenty years' time the shade and loss of light caused by the tree could sour neighbourly relations. Therefore, unless you have a very large garden it would be better to choose more appropriately sized trees.

Best Trees for a Small Garden

Fruit Trees: I would always recommend fruit trees for a small garden: they possess a wide range of good qualities: dappled shade, good habitat for wildlife, lovely to look at and sit under, whilst also providing fresh seasonal fruit. My favourite apple is 'Discovery' – with her numerous early red apples, she is hard to beat, but there are many others depending on your taste and needs; good nurseries and garden centres will be able to advise you. With all fruit trees, it is important to know the root stock: this will determine the eventual size of the tree. For fruit trees of 12–15ft height, choose the following rootstocks: apple – 'MM106', pear – 'Quince A', plum – 'St. Julian A'. For smaller trees of around 9–12ft, choose: apple – 'M26', pear – 'Quince C' and plum – 'Pixy'. There are rootstocks both larger and smaller than these – again, just ask at the nursery or garden centre.

Nut Trees: For a lovely medium to large tree (25–30ft, if left unpruned) that both produces dappled shade, a good environment for wildlife and edible nuts, a walnut could be suitable (the most compact variety is 'Broadview'); if you have less space then a cobnut, or hazelnut offers the same benefits (10–12ft).

Ornamental Trees: The list is endless, and much is due to taste – I personally love the lime-greens of acer Palmatum varieties, the purple of the Cercis 'Forest Pansy', and the white blossom and Autumn colour of the amelanchier – partly because of their leaf textures and the dappled shade they produce, but also because they change throughout the year. This means that they offer a 'new view' every season and perhaps allow me to glimpse the being of the tree as she moves (like us) through the cycle of the year.

I end with a last thought from Glennie Kindred:

> *"By developing special relationships with trees, we begin to see them as good friends who we get to know through all the different seasons, returning to visit them year after year as we gather their fruits, leaves and flowers for medicine or to make jams or drinks, as we use their wood with conscious thanks for their gifts. We can also sit with trees and soak up the wisdom they have to teach us if we slow down and ask for their guidance and help."*

(July 2023)

AUGUST
Harvest

Taking in the gifts of Summer, movement, compost (again!) and balance in our garden work.

LAMMAS, THE FESTIVAL OF FIRST FRUITS

Throughout July, I have been enjoying the gentle movement of meadow flowers, the bold strong colours of perennials like phlox, verbena and dahlia, as well as the as yet uncut hedges. From Midsummer (June 21st) to Lammas (1st August), I feel I am invited to take part in this dreamy exhalation and movement of Nature up into the Summer sky, and although some people feel the need to tidy everything the moment Midsummer has arrived, I would argue that we should hold back and enjoy these six weeks as a gift. Of course, some hedges might need a light trim, as will some flower beds and meadows where access is required or plants become ugly; but on the whole I try to relax a little and breathe out with Nature, enjoying the movement and feeling of gentle ripening. Throughout July, meadows are often at their peak of beauty, as are most flower beds – and the gentle movement of hedges (perhaps trimmed very lightly) exemplify this mood.

With the arrival of August, however, the work of tidying begins. The first small fruits of the apples will be ripening and even falling; therefore, I need to begin cutting the meadows below them. Hedges will indeed now be looking wild; a trim is necessary now that the danger of disturbing most nesting birds has passed (but please still check as some robins and blackbirds will be on their second brood). Some flower beds will be needing attention: dead-heading and pruning of anything that looks untidy. The mood of Lammas is one of transition, of change – both outwardly in my garden work, but also in an inward way: I am asked to reflect and to begin internalising the gifts of Summer. Glennie Kindred sums this up delightfully in her book, *The Earth's Cycle of Celebration*:

> "Lammas is the seasonal peak of high Summer and, as with all cross-quarter festivals, it is the point when we must respond to the changes which are coming. The grain harvest is being gathered in, representing for us both the food which will sustain us throughout the Winter, and the seed, which will grow again in the Spring to bring next year's harvest. It is a time to give thanks for the active grow period as the sun's energy begins to wane. We turn once again to face our inner selves, assimilating and understanding on deeper levels what we have manifested."

If I can find a way to connect to such moods throughout the year – moods which are celebrated through the seasonal festivals – I will, to a large extent, be guided in my garden work. This guidance will not have a dogmatic, scientific 'textbook' quality, but rather will be artistic and living, in harmony with the out-breathing and in-breathing of the Earth. I suspect that this cycle of celebration can be found in all spiritual streams: Celtic, Christian, Jewish, Buddhist, Hindu, Moslem, Shamanic (and more!), because they each draw their inspiration from the living Earth, her breathing, and her reflection in us.

'No-Mow May' Update

Last month, I wrote about leaving an area of lawn to bloom into a 'mini-meadow', following the concept of 'No-Mow May', and I wondered how long this might last … Well, in the middle of July, I mowed most of it. This was for two reasons: 1) it was getting quite tall and it would soon need more than a normal lawnmower to cut it; and 2) I wanted to regain the contrast of a shorter lawn with the still full meadows nearby. However, I still left one irresistible island of flowers within the lawn and the rest I cut on the highest setting; I am hoping that if I now mow only every two weeks, some of the beautiful low clovers and other flowers will soon return, and with them the innumerable bees and other insects …

(August 2022)

MOVEMENT IS LIFE – THE GARDEN IN AUGUST

"The flowers talk when the wind blows over them."

– Ralph Waldo Emerson.

Lammas time, at the beginning of August, is generally the time when I start to cut flower meadows. I begin with a few areas below fruit trees, because this is when the first small apples, pears or plums begin to fall to the ground and might otherwise be overlooked in the long grass. Invariably, the cutting of the meadow is accompanied by a tinge of sadness: although it looks neat and tidy and obviously very beneficial for the fruit, I feel a little bereft. Aside from the loss of the wildflowers themselves with their myriad colours and forms, and the thought of the insects and invertebrates losing their habitats, I realise that I also miss the movement in the slender stalks of grass and flower. Throughout the Spring and early Summer, we can walk through these meadows and enjoy the delicious swaying and rippling caused by the wind on the plants: this movement seems so natural, so obvious, so alive that we often don't notice it until it is suddenly gone; I wonder whether movement can help us to access deeper inner processes within ourselves? Perhaps creating and maintaining movement in our gardens is good for our inner well-being, as well as for aesthetic and horticultural reasons?

We all know that physical exercise is good for our health, we also know that being near natural movement, perhaps by a rushing stream or by the sea, helps us find an inner soul peace, as well as offering us a chance to become more mobile in our thinking, more flexible and more open to other people's views and ideas; this seems to fit with the idea that movement is indeed life-bringing. I believe that we need to find ways of creating movement around us and within us and, as gardeners, we can add to this pool of movement; yes, we need to find the balance between too much and too little, too wild and too tame, excessive free-flowing and excessive control, but I think we could explore ways of preventing 'locking down' our gardens too much; and by doing so, we might enhance life in the garden and within ourselves. So, how can this be done? I will outline four areas where we can begin: plants, water, animals and ourselves.

Beginning with our meadows, I would suggest a gradual approach with the judicious cutting around Lammas outlined above, followed by a light mowing regime over August and September. Not only will this be easier inwardly – we don't have to experience a complete and immediate loss of movement, but rather a gradual coming to terms with the cycle of the year as it moves towards Autumn – it will also help small insects, frogs and mice to remain in at least a part of their habitat for longer. Additionally, many meadow flowers (orchids and devil's-bit scabious, for example) only seed in the Autumn, so they will also be helped. With hedges, I would suggest a quick light trim in early Summer to allow access and light and a bit of tidiness, but wait for October to do the harder pruning. Not only will this save us time, but it will also cause minimal disturbance to late nesting or newly fledged birds. Also, the hedge will be allowed to still move a little, to offer its gentle life-bringing swaying: hedges are basically rows of trees kept artificially shortened – and one of the wonderful qualities of trees is their graceful movements; why don't we honour and respect that, for the trees' sake and for ours? Planting a tree itself is of course a wonderful way of bringing movement into our gardens – all trees express the movement of the wind in their branches in different ways. Which tree to plant is dependent on space and your personal choice, but I would generally choose a native tree like rowan, hazel, oak or cherry because of the diversity of insect life they host (see below). If we don't have room for trees or meadows, we can still design our flower beds with movement in mind: elegant swaying purple verbenas, ornamental grasses that ripple in the wind, plus many other tall or open herbaceous plants: soaring foxgloves and hollyhocks, feathery larkspur and gently flowing lavenders; most nurseries stock a good range – perhaps visit on a breezy day and see who waves loudest?!

Water is a wonderful way of bringing movement into our gardens. The simplest thing we can do is make a bird bath – birds really love them, and we do too – the splashing of a bird in a shallow pond or container often brings me a surprising feeling of happiness and contentment. If we have a small pond, we can incorporate a waterfall or fountain – although artificial, we are mimicking the glory of flowing, moving water, bringing with it the inner experiences outlined above. Going a step further, we could incorporate a flowform – with their intriguing figure-of-eight movement, these water sculptures have been designed to replicate the flow and sound of natural water, again with the aim of bringing health to ourselves and, interestingly, also to the water itself. There are quite a few flowforms in and around Forest Row – the Ashdown Forest Health Centre has three in its inner courtyard garden, and both Tablehurst and Plaw Hatch farms have a series used for stirring biodynamic preparations.

Birds and insects bring a further layer of movement to our gardens, this time in the air around our plants – we could make provision for them with good nesting boxes and habitats for birds, all-year-round food, and a planting design that encourages them. Alongside bird feeders, we can plant food sources like teasels and blackberries for birds and nectar-rich plants for bees – for example wild marjoram, lavender and salvias, as well as native trees and shrubs that host insects more plentifully than non-native species. We could provide cover for them too – which might mean leaving some grass long and some areas of our gardens wild into the Autumn and beyond.

We can also use the garden as a place for therapeutic movement/exercise. Many of us practice yoga, tai-chi and dance in our gardens and perhaps we sense that as well as being of benefit to ourselves, it might also help us find a deeper connection to Nature around us. All indigenous cultures use movement and dance in some way as a sacred pathway to the Spirit in Nature, and I am sure that movement practices carried out in our gardens can replicate this reverential and life-bringing quality. Eurythmy, the art of movement developed by Rudolf Steiner, is another way of bringing the inner truths of life into expression through movement. It is both therapeutic and artistic, and additionally, in mainland Europe, has been developed as a way of helping plants to grow healthier with encouraging results in both yield and quality. I have worked with eurythmy and plant connection over several years, and it is my experience that by developing a 'language' with and for plants, particularly trees, I have found a subtle and living connection to them. For me, this feels like an inspiring way of offering back to Nature what she has given us – recognising and honouring her movements and returning them in a living dialogue (see appendix 1 – *Eurythmy and Nature*).

Moshe Feldenkrais, the creator of the mindful movement therapy, the Feldenkrais Method, once said: *"Movement is life. Without movement, life would be impossible,"* hinting that it can feed us with an inner energy; in these times of uncertainty and stasis, I believe this is an important thought to hold onto, and as gardeners we have many possibilities to bring this about.

(August 2021)

COMPOST – THE HEART OF THE GARDEN

Last month I wrote about changing our attitude to garden 'rubbish' and mentioned that the best place to put weeds, grass and leaves is the compost heap. This month I would like to go into this subject in a little more detail: it is no exaggeration to say that the compost heap is the heart of the garden as it really does bring circulation, warmth and life.

As mentioned above, composting is one of the best ways to recycle material in the garden, thus creating a beneficial circulation of organic matter. This, however, is secondary to the main aim – which is to bring added 'life' to the compost and subsequently to our garden and its plants. This would be the way to think of the compost heap – through our work of combining, mixing and adding, which will be described below, we are 'adding value' to what Nature has given us. Whoever has stood next to a good working compost heap

– not too wet or dry, nor too hot or cold – will experience a kind of calm but dynamic balance as the materials within it gently decompose; it is warm and gives off a healthy odour. If the heap does not appear like this then it may be out of balance, the most important conditions to bring optimum balance and life potential will be listed below. Following this will be a brief description of the different composting systems.

Conditions

1. Aim for a good balance between wet and dry material. An ideal balance would be a third grass cuttings, a third leafy weeds, a third leaves/shredded prunings. In very dry weather, it might be necessary to water your heap; in wet weather, covering with a semi-permeable fleece may be necessary.

2. In addition to the core elements above, add fruit and vegetable peelings and animal manure, if possible. The manure can be from horses, chickens or, if you are really fortunate, cows, ideally from organic or chemical-free situations. All these materials are rich in nitrogen and act as a balance to the carbon in the woodier materials. Animal manure, particularly from a cow, is really useful due to the powerful regenerative effect the animal's digestive system had on the grass it ate, which will then continue working in the heap, bringing further vitality (never add faecal matter from cats and dogs: this is poisonous for the heap with toxins harmful for human health).

3. Turn or mix the materials. Mixing is the best way to bring balanced rotting into the heap. Avoid creating thick layers of dry material on top of wet. It is almost inevitable that at some time during the gardening year, the heap will become like this – it is then that it will be important to mix the dry with the wet using a fork or a spade; alternatively, the whole heap can be turned at a later date (into a space nearby), with a chance then to mix up the materials.

4. The compost heap is **not** a rubbish dump. Never put thick woody prunings over 1cm diameter in your heap, these should go in eco-heaps as mentioned in my last article. Never put in man-made materials: plastic, metal or glass; also, never put left-over cooked food in the heap (although this is technically compostable, it will quickly encourage rats). Compostable plastic, cardboard and paper is possible, as long as the first condition of a balance between wet and dry materials is maintained.

5. Add biodynamic compost preparations. These six preparations, made with yarrow, nettle, dandelion and other native plants, have been developed to bring the maximum life potential to the heap, which will then work on in your soil when the compost is applied. They can be added separately or can be sprinkled in a dry mix. These preparations add very specific qualities, such as stimulating plant growth, enabling extraction of trace elements, combating diseases, helping plants connect to their local environment, and more. They have been used for many years on the biodynamic farms at Tablehurst in Forest Row and Plaw Hatch in Sharpthorne. Anyone

fortunate enough to have eaten food grown on land enlivened with biodynamic compost will know the wonderful taste and vitality that imbues such food. For more information on these preparations, please visit my website or talk to someone at one of the farms.

6. Keep the heap in contact with the earth to allow worms in. Worms are a very important element in a compost heap, both helping the decomposition process and adding valuable nutrients through their digestion (if using a compost bin, it is best to use one with an open base; if rats are a concern, then choose one with a plastic base with small holes in).

Composting Systems

A) Heaps. The simplest system is a heap. Build it directly on the soil, perhaps 6ft long and 3ft wide and high (for a medium-sized garden of about 100 x 30ft). After six months, turn it into a space next to the heap; allow it to decompose further if necessary for a few more months before gradually using it.

B) Wooden frames. These can be bought purpose-built or homemade with pallets: for a medium garden I would suggest at least two with dimensions of 4 x 4 x 4ft. The advantage of these is that the material is held in place, so it looks tidier but the compost still ideally needs to be turned.

C) Plastic compost bins. These are useful where space is at a premium; here one cannot really turn the material, so it is important to add a good balance of wet/dry material at all times.

D) Tumblers. Again, best for a small garden, with the added advantage of being able to mix the material. As there is no contact with the soil, it would be important to add some worms (either from a supplier of compost worms or perhaps from a friend's heap).

In conclusion: be patient and observant. A compost heap will take about 6–9 months to mature and will need attention and interest throughout this time; but caring for the heart of the garden is a fascinating process and well worth the effort.

(August 2020)

FINDING BALANCE IN THE GARDEN

"Your deepest presence is in every small contracting and expanding, the two as beautifully balanced and coordinated as bird wings."

– Rumi.

A friend and colleague recently said that gardening is above all an experiment: there is never a correct way to garden; rather it is a process of trial and error, sometimes being too drastic, sometimes being too timid. Moving between these two poles of gardening, I might come to a feeling of balance, of 'just rightness', whilst knowing, of course, that the balance will be fleeting because gardens, like life, continually move on. Below are some examples of the way I have been experimenting with this idea of 'finding the balance'.

Pruning perennial ground cover at Midsummer. In one of my gardens there is a very long bed with mixed shrubs and perennials, fronted by the herbaceous geranium 'Wargrave Pink'. Whilst offering its many flowers from May to October without any demands, it does also become quite bushy and exuberant and can tend to crowd out other lesser plants and, if I am really honest, after two months, the pink flowers can become a little boring! So, this year I cut all the plants right down to the ground at Midsummer, using a combination of secateurs and a hedge trimmer (the bed is quite big!). For a week I felt I had made a mistake, the bareness of the yellow cut stems looked quite shocking in the middle of Summer, not something one usually sees. However, the new growth soon started sprouting and the gentle rising layer of fresh green, devoid of the ubiquitous pink, was actually welcome and enjoyable – reminding me of the pleasure that this geranium offers in the very first months of Spring.

Cutting meadows a little earlier than usual. For many years I have advised that all meadows should be left until around the beginning of August (Lammas Day), religiously adhering to this advice in my own garden, but what if the meadow looks untidy before that? Should I wait until August, or should I cut it earlier? This year I chose to cut some meadows earlier, particularly those in shady areas, because the first flush of Spring growth had morphed into an ungainly mess. The results were similar to the geraniums above – a bit of a shock at first, but now I experience a calm spaciousness in the area which is quite pleasing.

Leaving some perennials uncut throughout the year. The general rule for perennials is that once they have finished flowering and no longer look beautiful, they should be cut back to the ground. Following this rule, I sometimes leave the dead stems of marjoram, fennel and purple loosestrife (my favourite water plant) to remain long into the Winter. This year, however, for some of the marjoram and the loosestrife, there never seemed to be a time when the dead stalks didn't look beautiful. So, I left them – and now the new growth is twining its way up the dead stems in a rather pleasing way, which of course is what happens in Nature.

Maybe these three simple examples can inspire us to experiment in our gardens, moving from 'hard pruning' to 'hard neglect'; it's an interesting experience that seems to have reflection in my life outside gardening, trying to find the balance between 'too much' and 'too little'. And a final thought: gardens are endlessly forgiving, we are allowed to experiment with them, to make mistakes, to move between the poles of the radical and the modest and to work with them in unconventional ways. In my experience, they will always respond kindly to this approach, welcoming our humble efforts to engage in the universal process of searching for balance.

(August 2023)

SEPTEMBER
Pausing at the Equinox

Meditation, lawnmower choices, seed saving and developing a co-creative partnership with Nature.

THE GARDEN AS A PLACE OF CONTEMPLATION

At this time of year in late Summer, gardeners have the chance to rest a little, watch the vegetables ripen and generally take it a little easier. Autumn is coming but it is not yet upon us. Perhaps we will be on holiday and have a little more time to enjoy the gentle mellow light that becomes increasingly sharper as the weeks progress; the weeds have slowed down but the leaves are thankfully still upon the trees.

Many of us have seats and benches in our gardens, generally they are used for entertaining (outdoor meals and tea) or for relaxing (sunbathing, reading), but perhaps they have another use too? Meditation or mindfulness is now a very popular everyday practice, useful for de-stressing and for getting things into proportion in our minds; it has been scientifically proven to reduce depression and a whole host of physical and mental ailments. I would suggest that meditation or contemplation, if carried out in your garden, say on a well-positioned bench or chair, secluded and protected from the elements, can be even more beneficial. The mere fact of sitting in Nature, consciously slowing down and breathing deeply without thinking about what to plant or which bed to weed is in itself a very healing experience, giving ourselves permission to just 'be'. After the busy-ness of the Spring and Summer months, I would suggest that now is a really good time to start.

Once we have slowed down then we can start listening and looking around us a bit more: the bees buzzing in the herbs, or the geese flying overhead – there is a whole world of Nature that we might not have noticed before. With joy and wonder we start noticing ever more smaller things – ants, twigs and buds, rocks, mosses, perhaps even grains of soil? This too is restful and healing, and as we observe more, we slow down more – a lovely feedback loop. By taking this process further in our thoughts and feelings, a certain quality might begin to arise within us, one that we might not often find in our busy competitive world. This quality is gratitude: gratitude for the plants and flowers around us – those which make us feel happy with their beauty, those which feed us. The trees: shade-givers, protectors, home to insects and birds who provide their morning and evening songs seemingly for us, and the different animals that pass through many of our gardens

– cats, foxes, hedgehogs, badgers, mice, rats, voles, frogs, toads and snakes (all recent visitors to my garden). We can even get microscopic if we want! We can look at the soil, its constituents, including the varied range of minerals and stones to be found – this soil which sustains all our garden life. By taking time to slow down, to observe, with simple joy and wonder, we naturally start to feel grateful for the living world around us. There is much scientific evidence to suggest that developing gratitude for the natural world alongside joy and wonder is an activity that has many healing benefits: physical, emotional and mental, providing as it does a very real sense of connection.

A final suggestion that could be practised alongside those above is learning to follow the cycle of the year. The main festivals of Christmas or Yule (at the Winter Solstice), of Easter (on the first Sunday after the Spring Full Moon) and of May Day (May 1st) are well-known to all of us, but there are other festivals much less talked about now, that traditionally those who work with the land around the world have kept for centuries: there are eight major ones in Britain (in order from December they are: Winter Solstice, Imbolc, Spring Equinox, Beltane, Summer Solstice, Lammas, Autumn Equinox and Samhain). These festivals are connected with the passage of the sun through the seasons and mark the inner reality and mood of the season. By joining our thoughts and feelings with these festivals, we gain another meditative layer for ourselves – a sense of connection to, and trust in, the seasonal changes. As we move into September, we approach the Autumn Equinox (on the 21st of September), also known as 'Autumn Quarter Point', Alban Eleud' and 'Festival of Thanksgiving' – it is the time when day and night are of equal length. I would like to end by quoting Glennie Kindred on the Autumn Equinox from her beautiful book on festivals, *The Earth's Cycle of Celebration* (which describes all eight festivals in detail). I hope you find some time to contemplate this in the weeks coming up, perhaps from your secluded bench?

> "Equinoxes are a chance to stop and adjust. Things are moving fast now, preparations and intentions for the coming Winter must be made. Summer has ended. The days will shorten. The cooler weather reminds us that we all must respond to this transition and change with it. This is the beginning of root energy, bringing rest and renewal in the dark. This is the chance for us all to go within and re-enter the dark womb of the spiritual world, which provides a strong foundation for our lives. It is an opportunity to explore and understand ourselves.
>
> This is a time for ripening fruits, nuts, berries and mushrooms. It is a time for long-term planning on the land and planting trees and plants. Within ourselves it is also a time to plant seeds, which will incubate through the Winter months and re-emerge in the Spring, transformed and renewed by their time in the dark."

(September 2020)

TIME FOR CHANGE? – PETROL vs. ELECTRICITY IN THE GARDEN

Last week, I replaced my last remaining petrol-powered garden machine – a strimmer – and with that change, my garden machine system is now free of petrol. This feels significant as, like many, I grew up with the joys and despairs of petrol-driven machines. I do admit to a slight nostalgia for the smell of petrol and wet grass, and the distinctive smoke from a two-stroke engine as it strims grass, cuts wood or mows steep banks (Flymos – all the rage in the 70's). Most of the engines were quite simple and the carburettor was easily accessible, meaning that field repairs could often be done even by relative novices like myself. However, there were downsides – I have many memories of standing in a damp field in front of a huge hedge, vainly pulling a hedge-trimmer cord to restart an inexplicably stopped machine. The sheer frustration and rising annoyance of knowing that the machine would probably never start without a 'good clean out', and/or the ultimate: the cord would break from excessive over-pulling! Both scenarios would involve a visit to the repairer's and because it was invariably the busy season, would require it being left for a week or two; in the meantime, the branches would remain on the hedge and the money would stay in the client's bank account!

Modern battery-powered cordless machines, although of course not infallible and immune to breakdown, are many times more reliable, and my cash-flow and nervous system are much less affected by the rare stoppages. The other advantages are that there is no oil or petrol to deal with (meaning that transport and storage is cleaner), the machines are much quieter and of course do not emit smoke, so sound and air pollution are reduced. The carbon footprint of a battery machine is lower than one run on fossil fuels, and although there are still unresolved ethical issues with the mining of minerals such as lithium for the batteries, I believe they are better for the environment than petrol machines. There are many brands available that use this technology, ranging from domestic to commercial quality. One of the most satisfying elements to these machines is that they usually have interchangeable batteries, which means that any machine made by a particular company can be used in their whole range of garden tools. This is useful also financially – because the batteries are not cheap – up to £300 for a good quality one. I have two batteries and, on most days, I manage to interchange the batteries between mowing, trimming, hedge-cutting, as well as finding time to recharge them (which is an efficient and quick process).

Overall, I really enjoy using electric machines and would recommend them for most garden situations. I don't feel too much nostalgia for the old days: especially being able to turn a battery-powered mower fully upside down to clean the clogged deck! It always gives a feeling of satisfaction as I remember the ferocious Parks Department foremen from my youth who would shout loudly whenever I lifted any mower a few degrees off the horizontal: "Don't do that – you'll flood the carburettor!" (Right tilt) "Stop that – you'll clog the air filter with oil!" (Left tilt). Elaborate and complex ways to clean the undersides would then have to be invented using either a couple of bricks or two people carefully twisting and manoeuvring the delicate machine to carry out the cleaning. No, I don't miss that!

A 'New Discovery'

The most exciting 'new' process I have discovered this gardening year is an efficient way of disposing of light, woody hedge-cuttings. In previous years, I have gathered my Summer hedge-cuttings and placed them carefully in the eco-heaps strategically placed around the garden. Of course this is fine, but even for the largest garden, space eventually runs out: eco-heaps take longer than I first thought to decompose (full rotting will probably take five years or so). This can lead to an ever-expanding pile of woody material that may outgrow its allotted space. The solution came from my father-in-law, Piet, who has for years been religiously 'mowing' his prunings (sometimes quite large piles!) and putting the resultant chopped green material directly onto his compost heap. When I first heard the various clunks and whirrs of woody material being 'mown', and sometimes 'thrown', I was not sure if it was a good idea, but the resultant chopped material is wonderful for compost. If one takes care with the mower and avoids the obviously too thick branches, I have discovered this to be an efficient and neat way of dealing with hedge-trimmings. I would recommend this system particularly for the light Summer hedge growth – it is not particularly woody and comes at the time when the compost heap is often full of dense lush nitrogen-rich grass: adding the drier and more carbon-rich trimmings helps bring a welcome balance to the heap. Additionally, the clearing-up process is simpler, more efficient and enjoyable, and if one is using a battery system, one experiences the satisfying flexibility of switching the same battery from hedge-trimmer to mower to leaf blower, all in the space of about ten minutes! A great 'new discovery' – thank you Piet!

(September 2021)

THE GARDEN IN SEPTEMBER – SAVING SEEDS

This year, as a way to honour the Autumn Equinox, I am going to try more seed saving. The mood of September is one of moving from the outer to the inner, expressed by the turning point of the Equinox on the 21st, where the nights now become longer than the days. It is a time when I am asked to recognise the gifts of Summer: and as a gardener, alongside the (hopefully abundant) harvest of fruit, vegetables and flowers, the other gifts, often overlooked, are seeds. I have to admit that I am not very practised at seed saving, but after visiting 'Seedy Sunday" in Brighton (a community seed swap taking place every year in February: *www.seedysunday.org*), I was so impressed with the quantity and range that I felt inspired to learn more. Seed saving is great for many reasons: it is an inexpensive way of having seed for next year, it keeps good (and sometimes rare) varieties in circulation, and additionally through seed swapping it brings an element of community to gardening.

The best resource I have found on the internet is the company *www.realseeds.co.uk* who offer a free downloadable guide to seed saving and also seed drying: well worth having a look. They also offer cut-price organic seeds for those on low incomes. The main tips are: 1) 'F1 hybrid' plants don't produce viable seed: most seed bought commercially today is of 'F1 hybrid', so check your seed packet before attempting to save. For the process to work, the seed should be 'open pollinated' where it is allowed to grow and reproduce naturally. 2) Choose only the best and most healthy-looking seeds, removing any small or damaged ones; and 3) dry and store them very well.

SEPTEMBER

'Realseeds' suggest wrapping them in an old stocking and placing them in large jars half-full of very dry (baked) rice. The rice will remove the moisture from the seeds which can then be safely packaged in an airtight container.

Below are a few seed saving suggestions:

Calendulas (Marigolds). The seeds of these annual flowers are extremely easy to save – allow the plant to flower and then set seed (which it will do very readily). The seeds will have small pieces of dried stem curled around them to protect them, either shake the stem gently or use gentle finger movements to separate them.

Runner Beans. I have been growing and saving seed from a lovely runner bean variety called 'Prizewinner' for over seven years now. I am always a little surprised and pleased that it always grows true – producing amazingly vibrant red flowers, followed by delicious green runners. I save the seed by allowing a number of the beans to remain on the plant, and let the seeds fully expand within the pods until the end of the season (around the end of September). It is important that they don't get wet during this time as they might rot. I then open the pods and choose the healthiest and largest, drying them carefully before storing.

Tomatoes. This will be an experiment as I've never saved tomato seeds before. According to 'Realseeds' the process is as follows:

> *"Allow the tomatoes to ripen fully. Slice them in half across the middle and squeeze the seeds and juice into a jar. Ferment the mixture for a few days by putting the jar*

in a warm place for three days, stirring the mixture twice a day. This removes the jelly-like coating on each seed, and also kills off any diseases. It should develop a coating of mould and start to smell.

After three days, add plenty of water to the jar, and stir well. The good seeds will sink to the bottom of the jar. Gently pour off the top layer of mould and any seeds that float, then empty the good seeds into a sieve and wash them thoroughly under running water. Shake off as much water as possible and tip them out onto a china plate (the seeds tend to stick to anything else). Dry somewhere warm but not too hot, and out of direct sunlight. Once they are completely dry, rub them off the plate and store in a cool dry place."

(September 2023)

AWAKENING TO NATURE

As I write this in August, we are basking in our second heat-wave, with the effects of this in the garden to be seen all around – burnt brown lawns, low or empty ponds and streams, small, half-ripe fruits already dropping and, in some cases, plants dying. Whilst it is undoubtedly depressing and sad that we may well have created this through our own actions, actions of many decades where we haven't treated Nature with the respect she deserves, I believe that times of extreme weather (be it drought, flooding or storms) can also serve as wake-up calls for us to act differently and prompt us to search for new ways of connection to Nature.

SEPTEMBER

Last week I held a short workshop in the grounds of Emerson College, where a group of twelve people met for three afternoons, practising simple movement and meditation exercises outdoors. Our aim was to deepen our connection to the living world around us, and perhaps get an understanding of what lies behind the physical. It was a gentle and inspiring time, each of us learning some new insight or experience – in a sense, listening to the voices of Nature and her beings and so helping, in a modest way, to bring about some awakening to what she might be asking from us. Reflecting on the workshop, I realised three important qualities were required: 1) a safe, protected space in Nature; 2) time to let go of our everyday thoughts; and 3) a willingness to work together as a group. Maybe we need to consciously create or design these conditions into our gardens and into our social life to facilitate this dialogue with Nature. Below I will list just three suggestions – a list by no means exhaustive, but perhaps they will serve as pointers for further enquiry.

The first: a protected space – trees are a good place to start. We all love forests, groves and single trees. These beings, more than any other in the natural world, not only protect us from the elements but can also offer us a secluded space to sit alone or with others. We should therefore protect existing mature trees and forests whenever possible and plant new ones at every opportunity. The second follows on from this: in these secluded spaces, we can provide seats or benches, as well as safely designed fire-pits, where we can sit and spend some minutes letting go of our everyday thoughts and tuning into 'Nature time'. The third is more difficult: choosing to work consciously with others – we often lead isolated, busy lives and have maybe lost the sense of being with others together in Nature. The eight Nature festivals of the year might be of help: the Winter and Summer Solstices, the two Equinoxes and the four fire festivals (Samhain, Imbolc, Beltane and Lammas) were traditionally times when everyone would come together and celebrate the turning of the seasons. I have written about these festivals in previous articles (including the fact that they complement and often align with all religious festivals), so I won't repeat myself, but the point is: just knowing that people consciously came together to celebrate in Nature, means that we can remember and re-enliven this, not only at the festivals, but whenever we want.

Choosing to meet together in Nature, with a reverent and calm mood, and in whatever form feels right for us, might give us space to ask the question: "Nature, what ails you?" The answer may not be immediately clear but I believe that, with practice, new and surprising solutions to the climate problems of today will be offered to us from Nature and her beings – solutions involving a co-creative evolution of both ourselves and Nature. I want to end with a quote from Karsten Massei, who has spent many years connecting with Nature and who offers this hopeful message from the trees:

> *"Fortunately, there are more and more people who can listen and are devoted to listening. We are allowed to speak again. Whoever can hear us will be able to notice what happiness and relief it brings us. What do we say to the listening human souls? We say: do not give up.*
>
> *Let nobody take away your conviction; look at the doubts but do not allow them to win the upper hand. For you are meant to know that the physical and spiritual earth have again come closer together. What was*

SEPTEMBER

separated for so long will slowly, slowly come together again. The worlds press into one another again. Let this news give you hope. You can walk more freely and upright because you know that you are not alone in the universe but protected and guided by the spiritual world. The angels have not given up being there for you. Do not believe those who try to tell you there is a nothing.

The spirits of the trees stand by your side when you stand at the threshold. They are your brothers that have been sent to you by the spiritual world to hold, sustain and support you, so that you remain standing and do not fall over. For to fall is, of course, not difficult; it happens relatively quickly and easily. We are there to hold you. Take this information seriously because it can lead you to discover further the meaning of the role we play in your life."

– From *School of the Elemental Beings* by Karsten Massei (SteinerBooks, USA).

(September 2022)

OCTOBER
Going Within

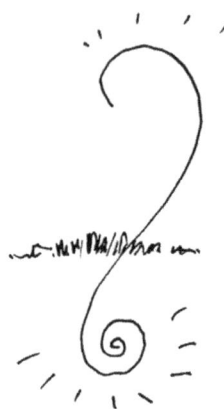

'Planting seeds within ourselves,' Autumn tidying, bulb-planting and the power of darkness.

AUTUMN IN THE GARDEN – RECONNECTING THE INNER WITH THE OUTER

Many of us feel uncomfortable with climate change and the depletion and poisoning of our natural resources but, equally, we often feel powerless and unsure how to change this situation. I believe one reason for this is that through 'civilisation' and the (necessary) growth of materialism, we have lost our natural instinctive connection to Nature. To find our way back to this connection, this 're-attunement' or remembering, many and varied small steps will be required, but as gardeners we might be well-placed to help. Perhaps if we can bring our outer work into harmony with our inner experiences, we will get an inkling of how we should be working with Nature in a kinder and more sustainable way? With the help from different spiritual traditions that have their roots in Nature, Autumn is a good time to practice bringing together some of these elements.

The Inner Path

In the Celtic stream, the Autumn Equinox around September 21st is celebrated as a time of thanksgiving and restored balance: as already mentioned above in the article dated September 2020 – *The Garden as a Place of Contemplation*, Glennie Kindred suggests that the period going on from the Equinox is the:

> "… beginning of root energy, bringing rest and renewal in the dark. […] It is a time to plant seeds within ourselves, which will incubate through the Winter months and re-emerge in the Spring, transformed and strengthened by their time in the dark."

I feel the quotation above is worth repeating for the month of October because it illustrates that the festivals are not just a one-day celebration, but are rather *time periods*. The mood of the Autumn Equinox therefore can be *acknowledged* on the proscribed festival day (mid-September), but can be *experienced* over a longer time period – in this case, throughout October up until the festival of Samhain at the very end of the month (see the article below: October 2023 – *Towards Samhain*).

In the Jewish tradition, this time of the year is not only a time of going inward but also the beginning of the New Year. The festival of Rosh Hashanah (literally meaning 'the head of the year'), calculated annually by the tides of the moon and can be anywhere between early September and early October, originated in the early agricultural practices of the Jewish people. There are many traditions connected to the festival, including apples dipped in honey to symbolise a sweet New Year and the baking of the 'challah' (a plaited circular loaf) to symbolise the full circle of the year.

Rudolf Steiner, the founder of biodynamic agriculture, had a way of bringing together many threads of spiritual knowledge, often related to Nature and the cycle of the year. His *Soul Calendar* – made up of 52 weekly meditative verses that reflect the inner and the outer in Nature and ourselves – does not discount other streams of knowledge such as the Celtic and the Jewish, but rather complements them and celebrates them. His verse for *Autumn* is a good example, where he writes about both inner contemplation and new beginnings:

> *"When I reach to my being's depths,*
> *Expectant yearning wakes and stirs me*
> *To find myself, self contemplating,*
> *As gift of Summer sun, a seed*
> *That warming lives in Autumn mood*
> *As germinating force of soul."*

The Outer Path

As gardeners, maybe we sense this changing of the year at Autumn, the new beginnings, 'the gifts of Summer sun' –

but how can we connect this to our gardening? Below are a few simple suggestions.

Composting: The gift of Summer: all the amazing lush green grass and weeds that we have collected over the Summer may well have filled our compost bins to overflowing. Now is a good time to move this into the next available space where (hopefully) earlier well-rotted compost from six months ago sits. This mature compost can be applied to our beds, and around our fruit trees. The newer compost can be mixed more thoroughly, teasing apart the areas of dryness and moisture, removing the forgotten branches, even the odd teaspoon from the kitchen – a nice activity to remember the previous six months, as well looking forward to the next ones.

Taking Cuttings: Autumn is a good time to take hardwood cuttings of shrubs, roses, as well as fruits like blackcurrants. To do this, we should select 25cm long pencil-thick stems of our favourite plant and trim them to just below a bud at the bottom and just above a bud at the top. These cuttings can be places in an area of the vegetable or flower bed where they can remain undisturbed over the Winter; it will be helpful to add some sand for drainage, as well as a natural root stimulator. As much as we go through a process of transformation during the Winter, so do these cuttings – miraculously sprouting in the Spring. The commonest and most successful shrubs are willow, abelia, spirea, hydrangea and most roses, as well as blueberry, fig, grape and currant.

Seed Collection: Many flowers and vegetables grow true from seeds, including peas and beans, marigolds and sunflowers – and at Autumn, they are easy to collect. The very act of seed collection places us in this magical place in time where we stand with one foot in the year just gone and one foot in the year to come, living in the place of balance and new beginnings. *realseeds.co.uk* offer a free downloadable guide to the most common seeds and how to collect them, it is highly instructive and free.

Reflection: Although Autumn can be a busy time for a gardener, it is a good time to reflect on the year just passed and remember our successes or failures. If a particular flower combination looked great then we can celebrate that by taking notes, sketching or photographing it. Equally, if a particular crop was unsuccessful or was eaten by predators, we should take note of that too… By next Spring we might have already forgotten.

These and other simple gardening tasks, which many of us carry out at Autumn, can be useful keys for connecting the inner with the outer. I would suggest the trick is to stand back a little, observe what is happening in Nature and what we are asked to do with it, whilst simultaneously observing how we experience the time of year. With luck, a little practice and inspiration from our own spiritual streams we might sense that the 'separated' becomes a bit more 'together' and that we feel more inspired and more hopeful in the face of the changes that are happening all around us in Nature.

(October 2021)

DO WE NEED TO 'GET EVERYTHING READY FOR WINTER?'

Autumn is making herself felt in the garden now – morning mists, dew and the first early leaves falling. Now is the time to find our relation to this mood, working alongside Nature with sensitivity to the changes that are taking place in our garden and in us. In earlier articles, I have written of the mood of the Autumn Equinox as being a transition from outer Nature to inner Nature, as the time when we move to the root energy of rest and renewal. However, although it is tempting to pick up our secateurs and cut back anything and everything that looks dead or dying in the hope that we can keep order and somehow 'get everything ready for the Winter,' I would suggest that Nature is asking us not to hurry this process; after all: Autumn has three months. The mood of this time could be summed up as 'gently allowing Nature to dissolve away and to accompany that inwardly.' With this thought in mind, I can offer a few pointers regarding pruning and tidying from my own experience.

Shrubs

Most shrub pruning takes place in Spring or early Summer, but there are some shrubs that benefit from Autumn pruning. Tender herbs such as lavender, thyme and rosemary are best pruned now: remove the flower heads and anything untidy, but if you want to cut harder then it is best to wait until Spring. Magnolias, lilacs and philadelphuses can be pruned before any frosts come: they generally require little pruning unless they are becoming too large, where simple removal of unwanted stems can happen. Shrub fuchsias can be reduced by a third to prevent wind damage. Hedges are best pruned in Autumn – I try to prune mine as late as possible, when there is no further growth happening, leaving them looking neat until Spring.

Roses

Both climbing roses and shrub roses can be pruned in Autumn. Climbers are still supple from the Summer, so they can be trained and bent more easily than in the Spring. After removing any dead or dying stems, look for strong young growths coming from the lower parts of the plant; if there are some then remove one or two of the oldest branches, and replace them with these new growths. Shrub roses and hybrid teas, etc. are happiest when pruned in March, just before the new growth starts, but it is often a good idea to carry out some Autumn pruning, which consists of removing dead and dying stems, and then reducing the plant by about a third, mainly to obviate wind damage that can occur during the Winter.

Herbaceous perennials

The television presenter, Monty Don, once gave some good advice regarding herbaceous perennial pruning in Autumn/Winter which has stayed with me over the years and makes great sense. It was simple: 'when the plant no longer looks beautiful, it is time to prune it.' If the plant has finished flowering but the seed heads are still beautiful then why not leave it? If the grasses have gone brown but still catch the frost then leave them too; if the teasels provide seeds for the birds, the same. What's great about this lies in the subjectivity which it demands, the pruning response is artistic and not scientific! When we feel the plant is no longer beautiful then it is time to prune it: it is our personal choice, reflecting our relationship with our garden and with the other non-human beings within it. Whilst of course there are horticultural reasons for sometimes pruning at a certain time, it is for me very freeing to have this choice as it connects us to Nature and her processes in an inward, artistic way.

Fruit

Whilst most fruit pruning is best done in Winter (apples, pears), Spring (soft fruit) or Summer (plums, cherries) blackberries and their cultivars like tayberries and loganberries are best pruned in Autumn. This consists of removing the old stems that have fruited in the Summer and tying in the new younger growths. Additionaly Summer-fruiting raspberries can also be pruned, removing the old stems and tying in the new.

Meadows

There is no perfect time to mow or scythe our meadows. Traditionally meadows were often cut at Lammas (1st August), as this was the time when the grass was harvested, followed by grazing from sheep or cows. However, most of us are now free of these considerations and we can choose our cutting time. If the meadow is in an orchard, then Lammas is most sensible: we can then find the early windfalls in the newly cut grass and have access for picking.

Other meadows can be cut later and, even if the flowers are dead, they have valuable seed heads for birds and also seem to have a certain indefinable and mysterious aura that still attract bees, insects and butterflies. They are also, of course, still beautiful in their death, particularly when coated with the first frosts. I therefore tend to cut meadows in phases, perhaps starting around mid-September with the first cut, and ending sometimes as late as November if the meadow has late Summer flowers, such as the beautiful blue bee-friendly devil's-bit scabious. As always with gardening, there is a 'treaty' to be negotiated with the weather, and sometimes it might be necessary to cut earlier than wished to avoid a flattened wet mass of grass that is difficult to clear!

By pruning, tidying and mowing our gardens in phases as outlined above, we can remove the 'shock' of suddenly losing the whole abundance the garden has given us over the Summer; and we are allowing ourselves a gentle movement towards Winter, more in tune with the mood of the season and our inner connection to Nature. Enjoy the Autumn!

(October 2020)

BULB PLANTING IN OCTOBER

The two sister festivals of the Autumn Equinox (on the 21st of September) and Michaelmas (on the 29th) mark a significant change in the cycle of the year. As we enter the month of October, the days become shorter, the darkness becomes more palpable, and we start to look towards the Winter with all its qualities.

There are many ways that we can mark this turning-point; one is to plant Spring-flowering bulbs. The symbolism of burying a seed within the dark soil, which then passes through the Winter, only to bloom the following Spring is both a simple and profound act which mirrors the inner journey that we travel during this part of the year. October is a good month for bulb planting: the soil is still warm from the Summer but also moist from Autumn rains, providing the perfect environment for the bulb. I will be planting wild daffodils – the 'Lent Lily' (Narcissus pseudonarcissus), as well as snake's-head fritillaries (Fritillaria meleagris) and snowdrops, all in groups within meadows and under trees. These plants are semi-native and are restrained in their flowering – for me, this feels more appropriate than some of the more garish bulb specimens. As I have previously written, whilst showiness in Spring bulbs has value, I prefer to stick to the muted palette of these more native species; they are usually grown in this country and therefore seem to keep me more connected to the environment and soil of *my* part of the world, helping me retain an inner connection to the intentions outlined above. Additionally, they bloom around the Spring Equinox and Lent, two further sister festivals, this time festivals of quiet expectation and hope, which for me can best be expressed in the garden with the humble beauty of these more native flowers.

Whatever bulbs are chosen, they must be planted at the correct depth and the soil compacted firmly above them, otherwise squirrels and other digging animals may discover them. Watering is not required as the Winter will provide enough moisture, and it is worth remembering that in the first year they will probably bloom later than usual, as they will take time to establish themselves.

A HAPPY ACCIDENT?

Whilst working in a garden recently, I came across a stunning bouquet of plants, squeezed in next to a rock on the edge of a path: a combination of a small euphorbia, a harts-tongue fern and a slender plantain dividing the two. It is likely that none of the plants were intended for this place (especially not the plantain, a garden 'weed'), but the group was special – so special that I kept coming back to take the perfect photo. In the garden, the combination of textures, shapes, colours and forms of each plant was absolutely perfect, particularly the slender upright stalks of the plantain holding everything together effortlessly.

Thinking about this later, I felt I had been given a valuable lesson: perhaps I should let Nature with her simple wildness into the garden more often? She seems to know how to arrange plants together often better than the best florist, with the maximum of beauty and the minimum of effort; and I should therefore always look and look again at the areas that I habitually and almost mechanically weed: the path edges and the flower beds, as there may well be a treasure growing, a 'happy accident' hiding in plain sight.

(October 2022)

THE GARDEN IN OCTOBER – TOWARDS SAMHAIN

October is an interesting month of the year, bookended as it is with the Autumn Equinox on one side and Samhain (pronounced 'sah-win') on the other. These two festivals (along with their Christian counterparts, Michaelmas and All Saints' Day) are both times of turning inwards after the Summer's harvest. The inwardness increases as the days become shorter, culminating in Samhain – the ending and the beginning of the Celtic New Year, taking place around the 1st of November. In the past, our ancestors who worked the land in Britain and Europe were very aware of this fact and took it for granted that although darkness was increasing until Midwinter, the seed of new life was already planted now. Adam McLean in his pamphlet, *The Four Fire Festivals*, writes:

> "The Celts saw the year's beginning marked by the descent of life into the dark of Winter, the descent of the seeds into the earth. With the same consciousness, the Celts reckoned the day to begin not with sunrise but with the sunset of what we could call the preceding day. Darkness preceded light. The night was the unconscious spiritual ground out of which the day grew."

Additionally, the awareness of death, which at this time of year is celebrated and honoured in both Samhain and All Saints' Day, belongs to this moment in Nature's yearly cycle. To find a way into this mood, below are a few October gardening tasks that reflect this reality, each one having an element of 'darkness' which perpetuates life. Perhaps by thinking about these activities in a contemplative way, we can feel into the motifs of Samhain, the festival of Nature's New Year.

1) Vegetables.
If you have grown beans, once the last have been harvested, don't be tempted to dig up the roots in the name of tidiness. Rather cut the plants down to ground level and leave the roots in the ground to release their stored nitrogen into the soil; the 'darkness' of the soil and the apparent 'dead' roots combine to create a wonderfully nourishing soil.

2) Fruit.
Monty Don in his gardening blog has sensible advice for apple storage:

> *"It is worth taking the trouble to store the fruit so that it lasts as long as possible. Only store perfect apples, which discounts all windfalls. Pick apples by gently lifting and twisting so that they come away easily in your hand and handle them as though as fragile as an egg to avoid any bruising. Store them so that they are not touching, in boxes or trays, somewhere cool but frost-free, dark, and not too dry. A cellar, shed or cool garage is usually ideal."*

3) Flowers.
Keep collecting seeds (as discussed in last month's article), doing this is a good way to experience that the 'death' of the flower in Autumn is actually a new birth and will bring new beginnings in Spring.

4) Lawns.
Don't rake up every leaf. Leave some patches of leaves in an area of the lawn that is not conspicuous, where the darkness and moisture can remain. This will invite many insects and earthworms which are, of course, vital food for our garden birds and, if carefully managed, could offer sustenance throughout a large part of the Winter.

5) Composting.
Cover all open beds and borders with leaf compost; this will create a warm, dark environment rich in nutrients ready to offer life to the new plants in Spring. For extra vitality, add the biodynamic preparation of horn manure (having undergone itself a wonderful journey of transformation in the earth throughout the preceding Winter).

(October 2023)

NOVEMBER

Fruitful Darkness

In tune with November, hedge pruning, beauty in death and the art of no digging.

THE GARDEN IN NOVEMBER

"This is the month of nuts and nutty thoughts — that November whose name sounds so bleak and cheerless — perhaps its harvest of thought is worth more than all the other crops of the year."

— Henry David Thoreau.

In November, we are invited to welcome the increasing inwardness and fruitful darkness celebrated at Samhain/All Saints' Day at the beginning of the month. Outer Nature progressively loses its beauty and form as the Earth continues her deep inbreath (which began in Midsummer) towards the Midwinter Solstice at Yule/Christmas. As a

NOVEMBER

gardener, celebrating this inward mood is easier said than done – the weather can be wet, cold and windy, and at the end of October the clocks have gone back an hour, meaning the work day shrinks, culminating in the shortest days of December becoming dark at 4pm.

So, what sort of tasks can we do to feel in tune with this dark, cold but transformative time of year?

Firstly, the leaves can help, falling now, sometimes slowly, sometimes quickly. Ashes in particular seems to drop their bright yellow leaves almost overnight; whilst the oak is more leisurely, dropping handfuls of their leaves every day from now until Christmas. One of my favourite gardening jobs in November is leaf raking on lawns: firstly, it provides a way of keeping warm in challenging weather and, secondly, I can make 'leaf mould' (composted leaves) which is a great garden resource. The leaves take two years to rot, so keep them separate from the usual compost, either in a wire cage, in a hessian leaf sack or a black bin liner pierced with a few holes. The resulting leaf mould can be used as Winter mulch for tender plants (I use if for covering dahlia tubers instead of the more labour-intensive system of digging up and storing in a shed), as well as a constituent for a home-made potting mix. Leaf mould and well-rotted compost (both sieved) can be added to topsoil and sand to make a good all-purpose mix (NB: I always leave some leaves in the wilder parts of meadows as well as in flower beds and under hedges – this provides shelter and food for insects and small mammals throughout the Winter). The whole process feels to me like a celebration of the transformative magic of Autumn. Additionally, there are some stunning leaf colours to bring the magic to our eyes too – particularly witch hazel, liquidambar, and many maples.

Secondly, in the vegetable garden, November is the perfect month for planting garlic. These wonderful plants actually need the cold spells of the late Autumn to help them develop their individual cloves: Autumn-planted garlic is always larger than their Spring counterparts. The small cloves should be planted every 10cm in rows 10cm apart and buried with just their tip showing (for the first few weeks, until the roots have taken hold, keep them under observation as birds are attracted to them and may well pull them out of the ground, leaving them undamaged and then ignored, but needing replanting).

Thirdly, in flower beds I continue to prune perennials as necessary, as well as weeding and mulching. The art of knowing what to leave and what to cut is an endless learning curve for me – every year seems to be a little different as I experiment with how the overall bed looks and the benefit or otherwise of seed heads for wildlife and beauty. For example, last year I left my marjoram flowers standing on their stems all Winter and never found the right time to cut them – this year they are all going down to the ground in November. Conversely, last year I pruned some large fuchsia bushes hard in December – this year I will leave them until March. I have to admit that the reasons for these decisions are not always conscious or logical but are rather based on feelings and intuition; perhaps I can hope that the inner processes taking place in Nature during November are mirrored in myself as I strive to co-create with her each year – a magical process always evolving and developing.

(November 2023)

HEDGES – PRUNING, PLANTING AND MAKING NEW FRIENDS?

Pruning

I generally prune hedges twice a year: once in June very lightly, and again in October/November a little harder. The June cut is light because there are still birds nesting at this time, and any disturbance should be as minimal as possible. A quick light cut with a good, *quiet* hedge cutter will cause minimal distress to any remaining nesting birds. Pruning in June also encourages multiplication of the leaf buds on the outside edge of the hedge, leading to more density. Unless the hedge is really formal or in a confined space, I would not suggest further pruning during the Summer, but rather allow it to gently grow with the Summer as any other plant would wish to do. Don't forget that hedges are made up of trees, often large trees (for example, beech or yew), and whilst we have taken this tree and forced it into a particular form, it actually wishes to be open, tall and blown by the wind. Perhaps the least we can do is allow it some Summer freedom! Once Autumn has really arrived in October or November and there is no further growth taking place, we can trim the hedge again. By pruning as late as possible, the hedge will keep its sharp architectural form right into Spring, a form now quite appropriate for Winter, reflecting as it does the crystalline sharpness of the season, and mirroring the stark outlines of the hedges' more mature tree sisters.

Planting

The best time to plant a hedge is at the end of November and December. At this time, good hedge nurseries will be lifting their bare-root stock – basically small/medium stems with really strong roots. I find these bare root varieties are much better than those grown in a pot – partly because they have brilliant root systems that are not constricted by a pot; and also because they are much cheaper! A good hedge nursery will have a range of sizes up to two metres, suiting all situations. The simplest way to plant a hedge is to create a trench, place the plants at the desired spacing and density (this can be worked out in conjunction with the supplier), and then backfill the trench with soil and some good compost, treading firmly around the roots. In dry Winters, it will be necessary to water the plants regularly (perhaps once a week) and, depending on the weather, this regime may have to be continued throughout the first year of the hedge's life.

Variety

The choice of hedge varieties nowadays is bewildering, but if you adhere to the rule of trying to keep as ecological as possible then the choices are reduced. If you need an evergreen hedge then I would suggest the native yew, privet or holly as alternatives to the ubiquitous non-native leylandii. These varieties will host more insects, and therefore attract more birds, and will make a positive contribution to the ecological balance of plants in this country. Alternatives to evergreens are beech and hornbeam, both native, which will keep their leaves throughout most of the Winter. Although not fully evergreen, they have the advantage of *changing* throughout the year: green buds in Spring, thick fresh growth in Summer and beautiful colour in Autumn all add up to up to a winning visual and ecological combination, to mirror the movement of the seasons. A final suggestion for a native hedge where formality is less important would be the mixed hedge. Good nurseries now supply a range of mixes of native species including blackthorn, hawthorn, beech, hornbeam, dog rose, viburnums, and many more – often they can be edible and all of them are of great interest to wildlife. These hedges can look slightly less tidy than the formal hedge, but what you lose on tidiness you gain in ecological richness – in Autumn, a mixed hedge is a delightful mix of berries, leaf colour and different textures, possibly with the odd late rose. If your garden is large enough then you could also consider allowing one or two of the plants to become trees – a simple way to increase tree numbers.

Making New Friends?

Britain has possibly the largest number of garden hedges in Europe, reflecting our wish for privacy and protection. Although this is on the whole a good thing, it can be a problem. All hedges tell two stories: privacy for you may mean overpowering darkness for your neighbour! Hedges are truly a reflection of the consciousness of today: we want and need something for ourselves, to feel protected and secure, we feel it is our sovereign right, but by exerting this right to the exclusion of all else, we may forget the other. If you look on the gov.uk website, there is a surprising amount written about disputes between neighbours regarding hedges; and as a gardener for more than 35 years, I can attest it is a very common problem. However, a few simple tips can help for good relations: the main one would be to keep your hedges low and regularly trimmed. For most situations a height of two metres is adequate, any higher will block out light for yourself and your neighbour; plus, a tall hedge is expensive to prune as it involves a large amount of ladder work. Please never trim just half your hedge top: if you can reach right over to your neighbour's side then I would always advise finishing the cut. There are three reasons for this: one, it will look much better immediately (without having to wait perhaps weeks or longer for the other half to be done); two, it will make your neighbour happy; and three, next year they may be inclined to prune the whole top themselves, to repay your kindness. A final thought: if you can't reach right over the top but have time and energy, why not go round to your neighbour's and ask if you can prune it from their side? Radical perhaps, but I have met some very interesting people on the other side of a hedge; and in these times, for me at least, meeting interesting people (and making them happy at the same time) seems like a good idea!

(November 2020)

WINTER SEED HEADS

"And I will show that there is no imperfection in the present,
And can be none in the future,
And I will show that whatever happens to anybody it may be turn'd to beautiful results,
And I will show that nothing can happen more beautiful than death,

And I will thread a thread through my poems that time and events are compact,
And that all the things of the universe are perfect miracles, each as profound as any."
– Walt Whitman.

Although the great American poet, Walt Whitman, was writing about *human* life and death in the above poem, I feel inspired by the idea that these sentiments can also be transposed to our gardens. In recognition that November is traditionally the time where we have the closest connection to the world of death and dying, here are five garden plants that for me encapsulate this quality of beauty in death. As well as often being strikingly beautiful, plants with interesting seed heads that stand well over Autumn and Winter are a good source of food for birds and provide habitats for numerous insects such as spiders. They should have a place in every garden.

Fennel

The soft, feathery billows of green foliage and yellow aniseed-perfumed flowers of fennel are transformed during Autumn into a real eye-catching gem. The dead flower heads can remain standing until early Spring, and the sight of fennel on a frosty morning with the sun low over the flower bed, is hard to beat.

Honesty

The delicate oval seed heads of honesty are preceded by pink or white flowers that are a good addition to the wild garden as they are a very attractive to bees. The Winter seed heads look particularly lovely when backlit by the sun and are useful for dried flower arrangements, lasting for many months indoors.

Teasel

If you have a meadow, then chances are that you will have teasels, as they are prolific self-seeders. These upright purple flower cones, adding good form to the Summer meadow, gently change to a dry brown spiky brush in the Winter. In the Summer, the flowers are magnets for bees; whilst in the Winter, the seed heads are irresistible to goldfinches, as well as adding an unusual and attractive element to the Winter garden.

Grasses

There are now many grasses available for beautiful prairie-style low-maintenance flower beds. Their upright simplicity adds elegance and calm to such flower beds, and this serene beauty can continue right through Winter until the new growths starts again in Spring. Like fennel, grasses such as Calamagrostis, Miscanthus and others are sublimely spectacular when frosted.

Sunflowers

Following the dramatic glory of the yellow sunflower throughout the late Summer, a rosette of many perfectly formed sunflower seeds remains for many months, providing welcome food for many birds, especially blue tits. If the head becomes a bit forlorn and soggy then a tip would be to cut the head off and hang it on the bird table or a branch, allowing the cold and drying winds to keep the seeds from rotting.

These five are just suggestions, there are many more – perhaps experiment with flowers that are traditionally cut down in the Autumn by asking: 'I wonder what this plant looks like when it is dead?' A pleasant surprise may be waiting …

(November 2022)

THINK BEFORE YOU DIG

Five Benefits of the 'No-dig' Gardening System

During my career as a gardener, I have slowly become converted to the idea of the 'no-dig' garden. It has been a gradual journey for me, letting go of ingrained habits and concepts from the past, as science develops and new ideas come into existence. Below are five reasons why I feel it is good not to dig, as well as some situations that I feel still require digging.

1) Healthy plant communities. Over the last decade, science has made enormous discoveries in relation to the structure of the soil and in particular the minute and dense network of mycelia that thread their way through the topsoil (generally the first 3 or 4 inches in a garden). These mycelia or fungal networks connect the root systems of plants and are intrinsic to healthy soil, allowing communication between plants in many ways, including facilitating the sharing of nutrients between each other. Every time we dig the soil, we damage and break these networks (the so-called 'shattering effect'), reducing the effective overall health of the plant community above the soil.

2) Increased air and light in the soil. Contrary to popular belief (and to the training I received in the Parks Department almost 40 years ago), regular turning of the soil with a spade or hoe does not improve the soil structure by allowing air and light in. In a healthy soil, air and light enters primarily through the activity of earthworms and other burrowing creatures. If we are constantly cultivating the soil then we are destroying these natural 'ventilation shafts', reducing the amount of light and air into the soil. I have to admit that this is the hardest habit for me to break – I have enjoyed many hours 'spuddling' – a Hampshire term for lightly turning over the soil of a flower bed to create a pleasing visual effect. Interestingly, I recently looked up the dictionary definition of this term: "To make a lot of fuss about trivial things, as if it were important" [!]

3) Better drainage. Soil that has a large amount of mycelia and many natural air systems will be better at draining and will not produce as much run-off as highly-cultivated soil. Additionally, even in wetter weather, one can walk on the soil with less disruption.

4) Lower maintenance. Clearly, less digging and cultivating saves time. The question of weeds is dealt with by mulching – the companion concept to 'no-dig'. Mulching involves covering any bare soil with a layer of organic matter – compost, grass clippings or straw – and by doing this we reduce the areas of open soil where weeds can germinate. Additionally, we insulate, protect and nourish the topsoil below; the organic matter will gradually rot and will be taken down by earthworm activity and rain. The use of cover crops – green manures in the vegetable garden, and ground-cover plants in the flower garden – works in a similar way.

5) Reduced carbon emissions. This is the buzzword of our time, and I find it so fascinating to realise that digging exposes soil microorganisms to excess oxygen and sunlight, accelerating the loss of stored carbon into the atmosphere. So, if we disturb the soil less then we keep carbon in the soil and help in a small way with slowing down climate change.

Digging is Sometimes Necessary

Although I am becoming more of a fan of no-dig with every day, there are some circumstances when digging the soil is necessary; for instance, when planting or harvesting. If we really must dig, then we should make the disturbance as small as possible and ideally use a bronze implement (bronze is less disruptive to the soil than iron because it is not magnetic and doesn't rust. It therefore doesn't alter the electrical energy in the soil or leave decaying particles of iron – both detrimental to soil health. Bronze also slides into the soil much more easily than iron, disturbing the structure less).

If we are new to no-dig then I would suggest that we could experiment on a small area of our garden first – perhaps just one flower or vegetable bed. If we try it for a year or so and then compare the cultivated with the no-dig bed, we may notice the difference in the soil health, vitality and reduction in labour. Additionally, if we take advice from the many experts on this subject (Charles Dowding – the pioneer of 'no-dig' is a good starting point, either in books or the internet) then the joys and advantages of this exciting and fascinating gardening style may, despite decades of digging and spuddling, become our new normal.

(November 2021)

DECEMBER

Midwinter Light

Celebrating the Solstice, Summer's gift of leaves, the native hedge, time for reflection.

THE HOLLY AND THE IVY – MIDWINTER LIGHT

As we move toward the Winter Solstice on 21st of December, the days reach their shortest length, the weather is often cold and wet and there is little outward cheer in the garden. The Christian festival of Christmas of course takes place at this time – built upon the older Celtic festival of Yule, both honouring darkness and rebirth – as we in the Northern Hemisphere pass through the shortest day and longest night. Glennie Kindred, in her book, *The Earth's Cycle of Celebration*, has, as ever, something helpful to say about this time:

> *"Deep within the Earth and ourselves roots have been growing, bringing stability. The outer world has darkened and the inner realms can expand. But here there is a change of direction: from now on the days will lengthen. Being part of this cycle means that we can bring our inner wisdom out of the dark unconscious, to grow with the light. [...] Winter Solstice is an opportunity to come out of hibernation, be loving, generous and sociable, celebrate each other and being alive."*

As a gardener, I am always trying to connect inner spiritual truths to my outer work, so I wonder how I can find a connection with the inner experiences of Midwinter with what is living around me in the garden? Two plants that might help are the holly and the ivy. Both are celebrated in Christmas carols – the first, *The Holly and the Ivy*, represents Christ and his mother, Mary; and the second, *Green Grow'th the Holly* (originally a love poem written by King Henry VIII), alludes to holly and ivy 'resisting Winter blasts' and 'not changing their green hue.' Perhaps the reason they fit so well into both Christmas and Solstice celebrations is their qualities of staying both evergreen and strong, whatever the weather, and offering light and hope in the form of berries and flowers.

Holly

Common holly, *Ilex aquifolium*, with its shiny, evergreen leaves can be grown as a specimen tree reaching up to 20 metres high if left unchecked. Luckily, it responds well to pruning and can be clipped to a smaller bush or trained into a hedge. There are dozens of varieties, many of which have variegated leaves. Both a male and a female plant are required for the female plants to produce red berries, which appear from late Autumn to mid-Winter. This year the berries have been very prolific, and these majestic trees can be seen in many gardens and woodlands, literally glowing red! After the first frosts, the berries soften and eventually fall to the ground, becoming a source of food for overwintering birds. Sprigs of holly can be used for decoration during the Solstice: the attraction is clear – bright red berries and enduring green feel very helpful and hopeful at this time of year. If you don't have a large garden or access to woodland, there are now many smaller varieties available – both green and variegated.

Ivy

Ivy, Hedera helix, is an evergreen, native climber found in many woodlands throughout Britain, growing up to 30 metres. It is often thought to strangle trees, but according to the Woodland Trust, this is an unfair myth: *"Ivy uses trees and walls for support, allowing it to reach upwards to better levels of sunlight. It is not a parasitic plant and has a separate root system in the soil and so absorbs its own nutrients and water as needed. Ivy does not damage trees and its presence doesn't indicate that a tree is unhealthy."* This is news to me, and although I like the idea, I have to say that I am still a little wary of it in a small garden because of its vigour!

What is without question is its benefit to wildlife throughout Autumn and Winter: it is a very generous plant. Not only does it offer the last nectar for bees, wasps and hoverflies; but also its nutritious berries, high in fat, are eaten by a range of bird species including thrushes, blackcaps, woodpigeons and blackbirds. Additionally, it is an important food plant for many butterfly and moth larvae as they overwinter and can provide shelter for small mammals, bats and overwintering birds.

Equally without question is the ivy's decorative value during the Winter season. The evergreen, delicate, long-lasting trails can be used in many ways including door wreaths and shelf/table decorations and really do look good together with holly; perhaps understanding their great value outside in Nature during Winter will enhance our appreciation of these two wonderful plants as we bring them into our homes this December.

(December 2023)

LEAVES – SUMMER'S GIFT, WINTER'S HOPE

During the Autumn months leading up to Christmas, one of the main gardening tasks is dealing with leaves. Most of us have appreciated the wonderful colours this year, particularly from the native trees around us – the birch, the beech and the oak. If we are lucky enough to have a large tree in or near our garden then we can love their beauty as well as knowing that the leaves are useful in many different ways – but they can become a problem if we don't deal with them. Beautiful golden leaves over the lawn in November, if left until March, will become a soggy mess, preventing light and air getting to the roots of the grass and ultimately killing it. Leaves in gutters or drains are a serious problem for water management; if left alone they can cause major flooding damage – too many leaves on a flower bed will smother young plants.

This article will list some ways that gardeners can deal with these issues, but firstly we should look at the leaf fall process itself. All deciduous trees and shrubs drop their leaves in Autumn; the magic of this process is that the nutrients and sugars that they have collected from the sunlight over the Summer are allowed to return to the earth below them, feeding and mulching the roots of the trees and allowing the possibility of more growth the following year. Leaf fall begins in the Northern Hemisphere around the time of the Autumn Equinox (September 21st). Traditional land-based cultures speak of the Equinox as a time for us to start contemplating the gifts we have received in our lives during the Summer, leading to a digesting and processing of these experiences over the Autumn and Winter, with new hopeful resolves growing from this in the New Year. The Autumn glory of leaves is an outer expression of this magical process – a gentle giving back; the colours and the joy they bring are reminders of this. Maybe we can connect the two experiences together – our inner journey of harvesting, processing and giving back with hope reflected in outer Nature? The realisation that we are both doing the same thing may help us feel more connected to the Autumn months and the admittedly arduous work involved in leaf raking, clearing and processing.

Unless they are choking plants due to the volume of them, leaves that fall in flower beds, under hedges or in woodland areas of the garden can be left completely alone. They don't need to be collected or cleared as they will do the wonderful the job they were designed for: feeding the soil. Additionally, fallen leaves provide a wonderful safe habitat for many small insects and micro-organisms – so a rule of thumb would be to leave some leaves everywhere (even on lawns and beds) and don't be too tidy!

If we have only a small amount of leaves then it is perfectly possible, and indeed useful, to put them in the compost bin or heap. The dry, crisp essence can be really helpful in balancing the other elements in a compost heap – moist grass, weeds and vegetable waste. As always, it is a balance: too many leaves and/or not being mixed well enough with the other ingredients will create a matted pocket of leaves which cannot easily be used in the garden. For those with too many leaves for the compost heap, a special container or area just for leaves will need to be created. Leaves take a lot longer to rot down than compost (generally two years), so enough containers will be required to accommodate both years of leaves. There are a number of simple leaf containers that can be self-made: four wooden stakes in the form of a square say of about 3 x 3ft with chicken wire attached to them is a very adequate and sensible system, as are recycled wooden pallets with the same dimensions. In a large garden, a simple pile may be adequate (although these will tend to be a little untidy due to leaves blowing away). A fourth solution is putting the leaves in bags – either plastic bin bags or special hessian sacks. The advantage of this system is that the process seems to go faster: leaves may well be rotted enough to use after only a year. Additionally, they can be stored wherever is most convenient in your garden. Once fully rotted, the mineral-rich leaf mould can be added to soil in the vegetable patch or flower bed, as well as to potting mixes for seeds and young plants (sieving may be required).

In Rudolf Steiner's *Soul Calendar*, we are offered a chance to connect our inner soul mood with outer Nature in the way described above. One of the verses for early Winter conveys the mood of this time of harvest and processing, perhaps another way to imaginatively and artistically connect to this moment:

> *"There thrive within the sunlight of my soul*
> *The ripened fruits of thinking;*
> *The flow of feeling is transformed*
> *To self-awareness' certainty.*
> *I can perceive now joyfully*
> *The Autumn's spirit-waking:*
> *The Winter will arouse in me*
> *The Summer of the soul."*
>
> *(Soul Calendar – 1st week of November)*

(December 2020)

THE NATIVE HEDGE – A 'MINI-WOODLAND' IN YOUR GARDEN

> *"As he hurried along, eagerly anticipating the moment when he would be home again among the things he knew and liked, the Mole saw clearly that he was an animal of tilled field and hedgerow."*
>
> – Kenneth Graham.

We all love mixed native woodlands: the diversity in shape, colour and texture of the different trees, shrubs and flowers present, the range of leaf, fruit and seed on show throughout the changing seasons, as well as the sheer variety of species of bird and animal life that they support all add to the enjoyment of these special places. Although few of us have space to plant a native woodland in our gardens, we can to a small degree replicate it in a native hedge. These hedges originated through the practices of traditional farming, where fields needed to be separated into different areas for different uses, whether it was livestock or crops. They were planted using hawthorn and blackthorn (sloe), as these were fast-growing and easily knitted together to create a stock-proof hedge. Over the years, the hedges became colonised by other species – alder, field maple, holly, sycamore, wild roses plus many more, turning them quite naturally into mixed hedges. Additionally, the hedgerow edge became a rich diverse area hosting a variety of native wildflowers – cow parsley, meadowsweet, celandine, primrose, violet and countless more – the exact mix dependent upon the constitution and moisture of the soil, the sun and shade balance and the land usage of the nearby fields. The hedge itself became a haven for wildlife: nesting birds found protection in the thorny growth, insects found nectar in the flowers of the roses, the honeysuckle and the many other flowers, small mammals such as foxes, badgers and dormice (and moles?) enjoyed the protection of the root system and of course the fruits of the bramble, the plum, the hawthorn and the sloe.

As Autumn comes to a close at the end of November and Nature has become dormant, now is a good time to plant a mixed native hedge in the garden. Although planting is a decision that shouldn't be taken lightly (like all trees, they live long and can have a considerable impact on their immediate surroundings), the mixed hedge has many positive qualities. Seclusion and privacy are often the main reason for hedges (a sort of modern urban version of livestock separation!), but equally they provide protection against wind, rain and sun, and of course they bring a small slice of diversity right into our gardens – literally a mini-woodland with its own unique and specific ecosystem of plants, birds, mammals and insects.

Planting mixed native hedges today has never been easier: many specialist nurseries now offer a large range of mixed native hedging, all based on hawthorn and blackthorn to 'knit' the hedge together, but with different combinations of native tree and shrub species mentioned above. There is a mix for all garden situations: for example, 'bird-friendly', 'edible', 'horse-friendly', 'gin-making', 'species-rich', 'thornless mixed' and all are readily available; the nurseries usually have very knowledgeable staff and they can advise on each garden's specific requirements, customising the exact mix of plants to suit.

By far the cheapest option is to use bare-rooted plants, this means that the plants don't come in a pot but are delivered with their roots bare (carefully wrapped to avoid drying out), saving on postage and labour costs. Additionally, planting is straightforward – simply dig a trench, add some compost, and bed the hedging into the soil. These plants are available for planting throughout the dormant season from December through to the end of March. When planting, I would recommend for a single row hedge using three plants per metre, each planted 33cm apart; and for a double row using five plants per metre, setting the plants 40cm apart in each row with 40cm between the two rows. Remember to firm the plants in well and if the weather stays dry then watering might be needed.

I would recommend mulching the hedge plants with compost or leaf mould, this will help retain moisture and prevent weed growth; adding cardboard onto the soil below the mulch will provide another layer of weed protection. In the first year, a light trim in August will be necessary: this will encourage bushing of the hedge. In subsequent years, trimming in August and again in November will be required, once the hedge has reached its desired height.

And finally: new plants will colonise the hedge, both in the tree and shrub mix and in the wildflowers at the base. These new plants appear because the conditions are right for them; I would suggest not immediately removing them, but rather living with them for at least a season, just to sense and observe what new and diverse qualities they bring to your hedge. David Henry Thoreau, the American Nature writer, sums this up in his quote: *"It is only necessary that man should start a fence that Nature should carry it on and complete it"* – and by allowing the 'happy accident' to take place, the new qualities that Nature brings may well enhance the enjoyment of the 'mini-woodland' both for you and for all the different forms of life that share it.

(December 2022)

THE MIDWINTER GARDEN

As the days have shortened over the last weeks, I have been tidying beds*, cutting meadows, and harvesting. Borders have been mulched with compost, roses have had a light Winter prune to prevent wind-rock, climbing roses, with their still malleable stems have been pruned and trained;

fruit, vegetables and seeds have been harvested. The final hedge cutting has taken place, the clear lines or curves silhouetted against the sometimes amazingly blue clear Winter skies. Whilst I have held back in early Autumn, I now feel the urge to finish the tidying of my garden by the end of the year, somehow to make it ready, to prepare it … the question is – for what?

Some of us might say "Christmas" (25th December) others may say "the Winter Solstice" (21st December) and still others may say "Hanukkah" (the Jewish festival of light which can take place between late November and late December). All these festivals occur in the time of Midwinter and are festivals of light overcoming darkness. In December in the Northern hemisphere the light slowly recedes to the darkest hour on the 21st of December and then mysteriously "stands still" for a period of days (in Latin – 'sol' – sun, 'stice'– immobile). Equally mysteriously and sometimes quite suddenly in the new days of January the light begins to increase. These outer phenomena stand behind these festivals.

I wonder if this Midwinter tidying is a wish to create a space of peace and contemplation (even if only seen from my house window) which allows me to let go a little, to breathe out and to "stand still" for a few days? For me the outer garden peace encourages inner peace. Alongside celebrating what is specific to our own individual or communal spiritual path, the Midwinter festival (which can last from 24th December to 6th January – the so-called "12/13 Holy Nights") offers us this space; we have a chance to enjoy being with friends and family, have time to review the past year and look forward to the next. (If we pay attention to our dreams during this time, often quite potent and vivid, and observe the weather on each day of the Holy Nights, some suggest we can divine how the coming year might be for us both inwardly and outwardly).

Maybe these thoughts can sustain us through December, as we work in our gardens with the wind, rain, cold and ever-darkening days, raking and clearing leaves, pruning and tidying – perhaps there is a point to all this!

*When tidying flowerbeds, the principle of balance is applicable. We don't need to cut all dying material away from perennials: some leaves provide valuable habitats for overwintering pollinators like butterflies and moths and can also provide protection against frost. Additionally, if the leaves are not too ugly or soggy (like dying hosta leaves which can harbour slugs) then they can be left to mulch and feed the plant itself; they are designed to do this, providing the exact range of nutrients each plant needs. Seed heads are both beautiful in frost and provide a food source for birds – in my garden, I leave uncut both St. John's wort and purple loosestrife throughout the Winter. Other flowers offering seeds for birds, particularly goldfinches, are coneflowers (Echinacea purpurea) and black-eyed Susan (Rudbeckia); whilst, in the meadow, teasel and fennel (as well as providing stunning Winter structures) are also rich in seeds and should be left standing wherever possible.

(December 2021)

APPENDIX
Eurythmy and Nature

Eurythmy is the art of movement developed by Rudolf Steiner at the beginning of the last century. In essence it aims to make sound 'visible' using the body as an instrument; these sounds can be music, the spoken word or a combination of the two. It differs from dance in that the eurythmist is not moving their body 'alongside' the sound but rather they endeavour to allow the sounds to 'work through' the body. The body becomes the instrument, and the resulting movement is the expression of this sound. (For a more complete description of eurythmy, see the links below). Steiner developed two related but separate elements to this art: artistic eurythmy and curative eurythmy. The former is a performative art and the second is a therapeutic art which empowers a eurythmy therapist to work with the healing journey of another person through movement.

Whilst there have always been two elements to this art – one more 'outward'(artistic), the other more 'inward' (therapeutic) there is also a third emerging element which could be called 'relational eurythmy'. This has been applied in businesses and organisations ('social eurythmy') for many years, but in recent years it has addressed the relationship between humans and plants. For me, it seems to combine both elements of the artistic and therapeutic, being both outward and inward at the same time. In this dialogue, I sense that a beginning can be made in developing new forms of non-verbal communication with Nature. This form of relating is a 'softer', more co-creative way of connecting to plants and landscapes, and as a gardener, helps me find another way of awakening to Nature.

I am student of eurythmy, an 'enthusiastic amateur' rather than a professional. However the experiences I have had of relational eurythmy in connection with Nature (particularly with trees) has more than convinced me of the potential of this gentle form of communication; I would therefore recommend anyone who is interested to look into the subject further, ideally experiencing some eurythmy for themselves.

Due to the scope of this book the descriptions above are necessarily short, but further information is available on the following informative websites: *www.eurythmymovement.uk; www.eurythmyassociation.uk* and *www.eurythmyonline.com*

For information specifically on Nature and eurythmy, the website of the Swiss organisation 'Institute ArteNova' – *www.institut-artenova.ch* is extremely helpful and interesting, including a fascinating video on the subject.

ACKNOWLEDGEMENTS

I would like to thank the following people and organisations for their help, encouragement and support in the writing of this book. I am indebted to Katherine and Georgina, editors at 'Forest Row Local' until 2024, for their initial article request and for their constant openness and positivity for all subsequent articles. I am grateful to my employers at Nutley Hall, Songhurst and Crossways, for the opportunity to work in their beautiful gardens and for giving me the freedom to explore and experiment with different approaches to gardening.

Thanks to Ellie and Lauren for their gardening help and feedback to my first articles in Spring 2020, and special thanks to my present garden team – Dan, Freya, Dillon, Jani, Nadia, and especially Wolfie, who have all put up with my endless cogitating about the next article, and who also provided helpful ideas and feedback. Many thanks to Wolfie for the cover design! A big thank you to Susanne, my very patient wife, who often made article suggestions which I initially discounted, only for them to re-emerge a few days later as my own 'wonderful ideas'!

I am also grateful to the following people who encouraged me along the way – Susan Raven, Sevak Gulbekian, Lil Tudor-Craig (who provided the wonderful cover picture) and Ellie and Owen who provided some crucial last minute editing and feedback. And last, but not least a big thank you to Pete Gotto and the team at Green Magic for their unconditional 'yes' to this book, and for their patient hard work in bringing it all together.

ABOUT THE AUTHOR

Michael Fuller had been a gardener for 45 years, working in such diverse places as Southampton City Parks Department, the Goetheanum in Switzerland (the headquarters of the Anthroposophical movement), various Camphill communities for people with special needs, as well as numerous private gardens. He now lives in East Sussex with his family and works in three large gardens with wonderful employers and a great team of fellow gardeners. He also enjoys selling bronze garden tools and sharing his love of gardening through writing.

Over the past 10 years he has been training in meditative research with Dorian and Antje Schmidt applying his experiences of 'seeing behind nature' to his daily practical garden work. A lifelong student of spirituality, Michael is passionate about integrating the eco-centric spiritual streams of today's world into his garden work. For more information, visit *www.michaelfullergardens.co.uk*.

www.ingramcontent.com/pod-product-compliance
Ingram Content Group UK Ltd.
Pitfield, Milton Keynes, MK11 3LW, UK
UKHW042205031225
465679UK00001B/82